D1045790

Set design by Thomas Lynch

Photo by Joan Marcus

Kellie Overbey, Troy Sostillio, Nat DeWolf, Kristine Nielsen and Julie Lund (L. to R.) in a scene from the Playwrights Horizon production of *Betty's Summer Vacation*.

BETTY'S SUMMER VACATION

BY
CHRISTOPHER DURANG

★

DRAMATISTS
PLAY SERVICE
INC.

BETTY'S SUMMER VACATION
Copyright © 1999, 2000, Christopher Durang

All Rights Reserved

CAUTION: Professionals and amateurs are hereby warned that performance of BETTY'S SUMMER VACATION is subject to payment of a royalty. It is fully protected under the copyright laws of the United States of America, and of all countries covered by the International Copyright Union (including the Dominion of Canada and the rest of the British Commonwealth), and of all countries covered by the Pan-American Copyright Convention, the Universal Copyright Convention, the Berne Convention, and of all countries with which the United States has reciprocal copyright relations. All rights, including professional/amateur stage rights, motion picture, recitation, lecturing, public reading, radio broadcasting, television, video or sound recording, all other forms of mechanical or electronic reproduction, such as CD-ROM, CD-I, DVD, information storage and retrieval systems and photocopying, and the rights of translation into foreign languages, are strictly reserved. Particular emphasis is placed upon the matter of readings, permission for which must be secured from the Author's agent in writing.

The English language stock and amateur stage performance rights in the United States, its territories, possessions and Canada for BETTY'S SUMMER VACATION are controlled exclusively by DRAMATISTS PLAY SERVICE, INC., 440 Park Avenue South, New York, NY 10016. No professional or nonprofessional performance of the Play may be given without obtaining in advance the written permission of DRAMATISTS PLAY SERVICE, INC., and paying the requisite fee.

Inquiries concerning all other rights should be addressed to Helen Merrill Ltd., 295 Lafayette Street, Suite 915, New York, NY 10012. Attn: Beth Blickers.

SPECIAL NOTE

Anyone receiving permission to produce BETTY'S SUMMER VACATION is required to give credit to the Author as sole and exclusive Author of the Play on the title page of all programs distributed in connection with performances of the Play and in all instances in which the title of the Play appears for purposes of advertising, publicizing or otherwise exploiting the Play and/or a production thereof. The name of the Author must appear on a separate line, in which no other name appears, immediately beneath the title and in size of type equal to 50% of the size of the largest, most prominent letter used for the title of the Play. No person, firm or entity may receive credit larger or more prominent than that accorded the Author. The following acknowledgment must appear on the title page in all programs distributed in connection with performances of the Play:

Playwrights Horizons, Inc., New York City, produced
the World Premiere of *Betty's Summer Vacation*
Off-Broadway in 1999–1999

To John Augustine and Kristine Nielsen

BETTY'S SUMMER VACATION had its premiere production Off-Broadway at Playwrights Horizons (Tim Sanford, Artistic Director; Leslie Marcus, Managing Director; Lynn Landis, General Manager) on February 19, 1999. It was directed by Nicholas Martin; the set design was by Thomas Lynch; the lighting design was by Kevin Adams; the sound design was by Kurt B. Kellenberger; the original music was by Peter Golub; the costume design was by Michael Krass; the casting was by James Calleri; the production manager was Christopher Boll; and the production stage manager was Kelley Kirkpatrick. The cast was as follows:

BETTY .... Kellie Overbey
TRUDY .... Julie Lund
KEITH .... Nat DeWolf
MRS. SIEZMAGRAFF .... Kristine Nielsen
BUCK .... Troy Sostillio
MR. VANISLAW .... Guy Boyd
VOICE 1 .... Jack Ferver
VOICE 2 .... Geneva Carr
VOICE 3 .... Godfrey L. Simmons, Jr.

Understudies were Marc Ardido, Joanne Cregg and Carl Palmer.

In June 1999, BETTY'S SUMMER VACATION won Obie Awards for playwriting, directing, set design, and acting (Kristine Nielsen).

There are Author's Notes at the end of this volume.

CHARACTERS

BETTY — a nice, fairly normal young woman, late 20s. Sensible, does her best to be reasonable.

TRUDY — friendly, chatty, needy, rather desperate underneath. Bit younger than Betty.

KEITH — sensitive, quiet, mysterious. Late 20s. Finds it hard to be around people. Seems sweet, seems weird.

BUCK — handsome, sexy lout-hunk. Might look like a beach guy out of *Baywatch*. Unabashedly sexist, on the make all the time.

MRS. SIEZMAGRAFF — lively, vibrant woman, mid-40s. Oblivious to anyone else's discomfort. Auntie Mame-ish.

MR. VANISLAW — an insane derelict who exposes himself to women in bathrooms; naked except for raincoat and sneakers. A little scary, but also just insane. Happy in his way.

THE GROUP OF VOICES — 2 men, 1 woman. They laugh, they applaud. They live in the ceiling.

PLACE

A nice seaside summer community.
Maybe the New Jersey shore. *Not* a trendy, chic location.

TIME

Summer.

BETTY'S SUMMER VACATION

ACT ONE

Scene 1

Sound of the ocean.

A summer cottage, breezy looking, inexpensive but functional summer furniture. Pleasant, soft colors, inviting.

An upstage door leads in from the front of the cottage. Inside there are a number of doors, leading off to bedrooms — four doors in a cluster, one by itself. (Some of the doors can be implied in an off-stage hallway, if need be). There is a door off-left that leads to an outdoor deck and the outside.

Primarily a living room, but an open kitchen is also part of it.

A woman, Betty, age 29, comes in with her friend Trudy, age 28. They are carrying suitcases.

BETTY. Wow. This house is great.
TRUDY. Isn't it? I knew you'd like it.
BETTY. *(Going off to look.)* Oh, and it has a great deck. And you can almost see the ocean. *(Comes back inside.)*
TRUDY. I know. It's a comfy house. I love that. It's so great to be out of the city. The pace is so much slower here. Smell the air. There's salt in the air. It's from the ocean. I love the ocean. I am so sick of cement in the city. You smell the air in the city and you

7

smell car exhaust and those fat unhealthy pretzels that those venders sell in midtown. But here, it's all healthy. I can't wait to eat only healthy food. What is tofu exactly? Well, we don't have to eat tofu. We just have to eat vegetables and fish and maybe chicken, but not put butter on anything, well maybe on a piece of bread with some sugar on it, do you ever do that, my mother taught me to do it, isn't it gross, but it gives me energy, gee, I really love the seashore.

BETTY. *(Polite, trying not to offend.)* Trudy, I've told you I hoped you wouldn't talk too much on this vacation.

TRUDY. Really? *(Trudy tries for a few seconds to be quiet. Betty looks around, checking out the various bedrooms. Trudy starts talking again pretty soon.)* What day is today, Saturday? What a long ride it was in the car, traffic really freaks me out, everyone in these cars, trapped, unable to move, did you ever see <u>Fellini's 8 ½</u>, that's what happens in the beginning of the movie, but then <u>Marcello Mastroianni</u>, he's so handsome, why aren't there any American men like him, I'd marry them in a minute if they'd have me, but lots of men don't like it if you talk too much, but I could probably have my mouth wired shut, at least if it was Marcello Mastroianni … anyway, he's in this traffic jam, and nobody's moving at all, and eventually he just rises up and floats up out of the car and it looks like he's escaping the awful traffic jam, but then it turns out someone has attached a rope to his leg, and so he's really still tied to the earth, and it doesn't look like he's going to escape at all.

BETTY. Uh huh. Listening to you is like listening to the radio.

TRUDY. Really, I wonder if I should have a show?

BETTY. Now I want you to practice quiet. Pretend you're a monk or nun or something and you have to follow the Grand Silence. Can you do that?

TRUDY. Sure! Which bedroom should I have? Which one is closest to the sound of the ocean? I love to listen to the ocean.

BETTY. How can you even hear it when you're talking?

TRUDY. Well, I hear it right underneath my talking, it's kind of like they say if you have a puppy and you're training it to sleep alone on a blanket, you should put a ticking clock next to it and it'll think it's its mother breathing, but I don't think a puppy is that stupid, do you, and plus it certainly wouldn't work with a human, I'd either think, this is a ticking bomb, or I'd think this clock is too loud, I won't be able to sleep with this racket, maybe I should order a pizza. Isn't it scary about germ warfare?

BETTY. What does a pizza have to do with anything?

TRUDY. Well, you know if I was hungry. I don't suppose there's food here, is there? We probably have to go to the store. I love to go to the supermarkets outside of the city, the aisles are so wide and comfortable, and the check-out people say "thank you" and so on.

BETTY. Yes, we'll have to go shopping. I think I need aspirin. And maybe ear stoppers.

TRUDY. Then you won't be able to hear the ocean. I love hearing the ocean. I'm so glad to be away from the sound of the city. Car alarms. Has a car alarm ever stopped a car from being stolen? I doubt it. It just goes on and on. *(She begins to imitate various car alarms.)* Oooooo-oooo. Ooooooooo-ooooo. Waaahhhh-ahhhhh, waaaaaaaa-ahhhhh. Wuuuuuu-uuuulp! Wuuuuuu-uuuulp!

BETTY. Why don't you take a nap?

TRUDY. I just got here, I'm too full of energy. *(Looks toward entrance door.)* Oh, look, here comes another roommate, or maybe he's a serial killer, I hope not. *(Enter Keith. He carries a large shovel, and a hatbox, and a suitcase. He's 28 to 32 years old, fairly attractive, dressed in khakis and a plain sports shirt.)*

KEITH. Hi, I'm Keith. Are you Helen and Susie?

TRUDY. No, I'm Trudy, and this is Betty.

BETTY. Hi.

TRUDY. I hope you're not a serial killer, and that shovel's for burying people. And what's in the hatbox? Not a head, I hope. That's another old movie I like, _Night Must Fall_, with Robert Montgomery, he's Elizabeth Montgomery's father from *Bewitched*, isn't it amazing how many children of people in show business go on to have successful careers, like talent is genetic for real, as well as, of course, it opens doors for you if your parent is in show business ... well, he keeps a head in a hatbox for the whole movie, and then you find out that's what he's been doing. Gosh, you look startled. Is it because I've said something outlandish, or is it because you really are a serial killer and you're guilty?

KEITH. *(Looking startled.)* No. I'm not looking startled. Please don't look in the hatbox, it's private. It has ... hats in it. And I go everywhere with a shovel because what if my car gets caught in a snow drift.

TRUDY. But it's summer.

KEITH. Well … eventually it will be winter again. And plus, my car could get caught in a sand dune.

TRUDY. Uh huh.

BETTY. Why did you ask if we were Helen and Susie?

KEITH. I'm sorry. I meant Betty and Trudy, I guess. I mean, I've never met you, I've only met the owner of the cottage, Mrs. Siezmagraff.

BETTY. Oh.

TRUDY. Wow. You're really cute. Do you have a girlfriend?

KEITH. I believe in celibacy. *(Trudy stares at him. Silence.)*

BETTY. Well, that shut her up.

KEITH. I'd like to go to my room now. Do you know where it is?

BETTY. We haven't chosen rooms yet. Why don't we go look and see what we want. *(Points.)* There are these four together, and then that one over there by itself. *(Keith kind of bolts over to the room by itself, and goes into it, shutting the door behind him. Trudy sits down, stunned. She starts to cry.)* What's the matter?

TRUDY. I think he's horrible. What does he mean, he believes in celibacy. Is he a monk or something? And what's in the hatbox? And why does he have a shovel? Maybe he really is a serial killer. *(Sound of laughter, like on a television sitcom. Trudy and Betty hear it, and look disoriented.)* Did you just hear something?

BETTY. It sounded like a laugh track.

TRUDY. Oh, God, he's weird … he's brought a taped recording of people laughing. What's the matter with him? *(Sounds of laughter.)*

BETTY. I don't think it's him. *(Knocks on door.)* Keith, you're not playing a tape of anything, are you?

KEITH. *(Off.)* I'm busy now, I can't talk.

TRUDY. Why is he so weird? *(Laughter. Enter Mrs. Siezmagraff. She is 45 to 55, a vibrant woman in bright clothes. She has a large sunhat on, and sunglasses.)*

MRS. SIEZMAGRAFF. Hi, everyone. Isn't the cottage great? Have you chosen your bedrooms yet? I want the smallest one, I shouldn't really even be here, but my husband just died and we lost the house, and I don't really have anywhere else to live but here. Plus I love young people anyway. *(Laughter.)*

10

BETTY. *(Focused more on Mrs. Siezmagraff than on the laughter right now.)* What?

MRS. SIEZMAGRAFF. What was that laughter? Did you hear it?

TRUDY. I think it's laughter from a sitcom.

MRS. SIEZMAGRAFF. Oh. Well, that's alright then. So, are you surprised to see me?

BETTY. Well, yes, I mean, aren't you renting the house *to* us? Do you mean, you're going to be staying here with us?

MRS. SIEZMAGRAFF. Yes, isn't it a kick?

TRUDY. We're afraid Keith may be a serial killer.

MRS. SIEZMAGRAFF. Oh, well, I'll know when I meet him. I'm a very good judge of character, especially men's characters. My husband died of cirrhosis of the liver. Do you think he was an alcoholic? All my friends do. I could never tell. Sometimes he'd beat me, but you know, he was always sorry, so I always forgave him. Forgiving is important, don't you think?

BETTY. I'm sorry. I find that you and Trudy seem to talk similarly. Why is that?

MRS. SIEZMAGRAFF. Well, she's my daughter.

TRUDY. Oh, Mom, I didn't want anyone to know! *(Trudy slams off to her room. Laughter.)*

BETTY. You're Trudy's mother?

MRS. SIEZMAGRAFF. Yes. But we don't talk much because her father incested her when he was drunk, and I never did anything about it because I was co-dependent. I mean, what should I have done? Broken up the family and gone on welfare?

BETTY. Uh huh. You're Trudy's mother?

MRS. SIEZMAGRAFF. No, not really. Well, yes, but we haven't worked it through yet. She doesn't like to see me.

BETTY. Well, when you said your husband died, why didn't Trudy react?

MRS. SIEZMAGRAFF. She's very disconnected from her feelings. That's why she talks so much. Even in the cradle. Gee gee gee, ga ga ga. On and on she went, saying absolutely nothing. It was real annoying. We used to leave her alone for hours at a time, and just put this big clicking clock next to her. Wow, I'm starved, is there any food yet?

BETTY. No, we haven't gone to the store yet.

11

MRS. SIEZMAGRAFF. Well, when you go, get me about twelve bagels, I eat them all the time, there's no fat in them, you know.
BETTY. Bagels, right. You know, I just thought about something. Haven't you already met Keith? I mean the one you said you'd know if he was a serial killer when you met him. Didn't you meet him when he applied for a share in the house? I thought you met all of us.
MRS. SIEZMAGRAFF. Yeah, I met him. Which one was he? The big macho one or the sort of sensitive one with the hatbox.
BETTY. He's the one with a hatbox.
MRS. SIEZMAGRAFF. Oh, I don't think he's a serial killer. Do you? Does he say he is? It isn't Trudy who thinks he's a killer, is it? She thought her father was a sex pervert, and he wasn't. He was just drunk. So she exaggerates. I don't believe anything Trudy says, she's worthless. *(Calls out toward Trudy's door.)* No, she's wonderful! *(Makes face at Betty — "well, I tried.")* But I think Keith is fine. Don't you? Is he here? *(Knocks on Keith's door.)* Hi Keith. How are you? It's Mrs. Siezmagraff, I'm here to share the summer with you all, isn't that great? Keith? *(Back to Betty.)* Well, he's quiet. Gosh, since I'm here, there'll be one less bedroom. Well, maybe one of the people due to be here will be killed in a car crash. Although traffic was moving very slowly. Maybe there'll be an earthquake. Except we're on the East Coast, not the West Coast. Of course, there are earth quakes on the East Coast.
BETTY. Please, I feel you're talking too much.
MRS. SIEZMAGRAFF. Well, fuck you! *(Mrs. Siezmagraff storms to Keith's room, slams the door. Inside she and Keith both scream. She comes out of the room. Goes to another door, goes inside, slams it shut. Enter Buck. He's the "macho" one ... handsome, muscular, in jeans and sleeveless T-shirt. He carries weights and a six-pack of beer.)*
BUCK. Hi, there, I'm Buck. Where's the party?
BETTY. Well, this is it, I guess. Hi, I'm Betty.
BUCK. Hi. I'm Buck. Wanna beer?
BETTY. No, thank you. It's sort of early in the morning.
BUCK. Yeah? Think I'll have a brew. Hold this, would you? *(He hands her a weight; she holds it, it drops down to the ground due to its heaviness. Laughter. He opens a beer, which was why he handed her the weight. He hears the laughter.)* What was that?

BETTY. I don't know. There seems to be a laugh track in the house.

BUCK. Cool. Do you like flavored condoms?

BETTY. No, I don't. I prefer that people get tested first. *(Buck picks the weights back up, sips his beer.)*

BUCK. Yeah, but then they could go have sex right after the test, so you never know really, do you? When you go to the store, get me some condoms, okay? I only got twenty-five left. Where should I put my weights?

BETTY. I don't know. On the ground? *(Laughter. Buck comes up very close to Betty; his body is inappropriately close to hers. Very seductive.)*

BUCK. I mean, which room is mine?

BETTY. *(Flustered.)* Oh. Well, there are two left ... that one and that one.

BUCK. If you don't point when you say "that one and that one," I don't know which ones you mean.

BETTY. Oh, sorry. There's this one here, and the one at the end of the hall on the left. *(Laughter.)*

BUCK. Great. You wanna have sex?

BETTY. Really, I just met you.

BUCK. Well, if you change your mind, I haven't got my rocks off since this morning.

BETTY. It is this morning.

BUCK. Well, since earlier this morning. *(Laughter.)* That laughter is kind of annoying. Can you do anything to control it?

BETTY. I don't think so.

BUCK. *(Looks up; shouts.)* Shut up! *(To Betty.)* Well, see you later. *(He exits to his room. Betty is momentarily overwhelmed by the people she's just met. Almost has to shake off the strange energy. Maybe we hear the sound of the ocean again.)*

BETTY. *(To herself.)* Gosh, there's only one room left ... and there's still another person to come ... Abigail, I think. *(Phone rings.)* Hello? Who? Who died? Oh, a car accident. *(Laughter. Betty looks shocked that the laugh track laughed at this. Re-focuses on call.)* Gee that's a shame. Is this Abigail's mother? No? Her masseuse? Really. Were you in the car with her? Uh huh. Well, were you massaging her while she was driving? Really? No, I'm not saying you caused the accident. I'm just saying, I think a massage should be given on a massage table and not in a moving vehicle. Well, perhaps I am rigid. But I'm not dead either, am I? Hello ... hello. *(Feeling oddly bad, and even though no one is there any more.)* Sorry. *(Hangs up.)* Gosh, how strange. *(Laughter. Betty looks up toward the laughter. End scene.)*

Scene 2

Later that day. Trudy and Buck come in from outside, in wet bathing suits, drying themselves.

TRUDY. Oh, the ocean was so refreshing.

BUCK. Yeah, it was great.

TRUDY. Oh, I love being out of the city. It's so fresh here by the ocean. You know, where life began, with the fish crawling out of the water and developing backbones and then becoming monkeys or dinosaurs and then eventually humans.

BUCK. What? Yeah. You're real pretty, you know that.

TRUDY. Thank you. *(To herself.)* My father always thought so.

BUCK. Well, he was right.

TRUDY. He just died apparently.

BUCK. Really? That's cool. I mean, that's too bad. What do you mean apparently?

TRUDY. Well, Mrs. Siezmagraff told me.

BUCK. Uh huh. Wow, all this talk about the ocean is making me horny.

TRUDY. We weren't talking about the ocean, we were talking about death.

BUCK. Whatever. *(Laughter.)* Shut up!

TRUDY. Were you ever molested by you parents?

BUCK. Is this kind of foreplay talk? Wow, you're kinky.

TRUDY. No, it's not kinky, I'm opening up my soul to you.

BUCK. Don't do that. Open up your bathing suit to me.

TRUDY. It doesn't open up, it comes off. You're a pig.

BUCK. Oink, oink. You wanna brew?

TRUDY. Brew? You mean, beer?

BUCK. Whatever.

TRUDY. Cool, whatever, brew. I hate the way you talk. You're an idiot.

BUCK. I don't care. Let's just have sex, okay?

TRUDY. You're just like my father.

BUCK. Wow. Kinky.

TRUDY. It's not kinky, it's pathetic.

BUCK. Whatever turns you on.

TRUDY. Stop saying that. Nothing turns me on. I like Keith more than I like you. He's more sensitive. *(Knocks on Keith's door.)* Keith, do you want to come out and talk for a while. Buck is bothering me.

KEITH. *(Off.)* I'm busy now.

TRUDY. Well, can't you come out? *(Keith comes out with rubber gloves on, which seem to be bloody.)*

KEITH. I'm doing an operation now. What do you want?

TRUDY. *(Taken aback; tries to act normal.)* Oh, I'm sorry. I just wanted some company.

KEITH. Well, I'm sorry. Now isn't a good time. *(Laughter. Keith goes back in his room)*

BUCK. Keith is pretty weird, huh?

TRUDY. Yeah. What did he mean, an operation?

BUCK. I don't know. You know, what a doctor does. He must be a doctor. Or veterinarian.

TRUDY. Yeah. He could be a veterinarian. *(Knocks on door.)* Keith, are you a veterinarian?

KEITH. *(Off.)* I can't talk now. Leave me alone.

BUCK. Wow. I've got a boner. Wanna see?

TRUDY. Please, you're disgusting.

BUCK. Oh, you love it. Here, feel it.

TRUDY. Stop it. This is sexual harassment.

BUCK. Yeah, I love that stuff. Did you see *Oleanna*? It was this cool play about sexual harassment. I loved it when the guy finally punched that bitch. POW, POW! Right in the chops. That was a good play.

TRUDY. I didn't see it.

BUCK. I have pictures of my penis. Do you want to see them?

TRUDY. No, I don't. You have pictures??? Yes, I would like to see them.

BUCK. They're in my room. Hold on a sec. *(Buck bounds out to his bedroom.)*

TRUDY. I'm glad you're dead, Daddy! I'm glad! *(Laughter.)* What's funny about that?

LAUGH TRACK VOICES. *(Speaking as a group.)* It sounded corny. *(Trudy screams at the sound of the group speaking. Laughter. Enter Buck carrying a very large photo album.)*

BUCK. Here are my dick pix. *(They sit on the couch, look at his photo album.)* This is when it's only semi-erect. And this is a morning hard-on. And this is me pissing.

TRUDY. Mmmm, very nice ... I think I don't want to see any more pictures of your penis.

BUCK. Makin' ya hungry for the real thing, huh?

TRUDY. No ... that's really very far from what I was thinking. I think I want to become a lesbian.

BUCK. Cool. I could dig it with two chicks.

TRUDY. I want to talk about religion. Unitarianism seems a nice religion. Put your penis away, please. *(She closes the photo album.)*

BUCK. Oh, you're a tease. I'm so horny now, ya gotta help me, Trudy. *(Buck starts to nuzzle her. Trudy pulls away. Before things can go too far, Betty comes in, carrying several bags of groceries.)*

BETTY. I'm back.

BUCK. Hi. You get the beer and the condoms?

BETTY. Yes, Buck, I did.

BUCK. Cool. I got a ragin' hard-on.

BETTY. Really. Maybe you could get shots of estrogen, and it might subside.

BUCK. Yeah. You wish.

TRUDY. Betty, have you seen Mrs. Siezmagraff?

BETTY. You mean, your mother? No, isn't she here?

TRUDY. I don't know where she is. *(To Buck.)* Should we tell her about Keith?

BUCK. Keith? What about him?

TRUDY. Well, how he seemed when he came out of his room.

BUCK. How did he seem?

TRUDY. Well, he had on bloody rubber gloves. Why were they bloody?

BETTY. What?

TRUDY. Keith had on bloody rubber gloves.

BETTY. Goodness. Why?

BUCK. Well, to protect his hands probably. *(Laughter.)* Shut up!

BETTY. Oh dear. I have a queasy feeling about Keith.

BUCK. You're probably just horny. You wanna get it on? Trudy's bein' a fuckin' cock tease.

BETTY. You're totally gross. *(Laughter.)* In what way is that funny?

LAUGH TRACK VOICES. *(Speaking as a group.)* It was so true it was funny. *(Betty and Trudy both scream. Buck is also bothered to hear them speak.)*

BUCK. Shut up! *(Enter Mrs. Siezmagraff in beach caftan.)*

MRS. SIEZMAGRAFF. Hi, everybody. I just got stung by a sting ray. *(Mrs. Siezmagraff collapses on the floor in a heap. Laughter. Everyone stares down at her. Keith comes out of his door, still with his bloody gloves on. He joins the others in looking down at the collapsed Mrs. Siezmagraff. More laughter. End scene.)*

Scene 3

Evening. Preparations for a nice dinner. Candlelight. Betty is cooking. (The dinner setup is probably best set offstage, on the deck area.)

Mrs. Siezmagraff comes out, all dressed up in a floor length summer gown that hides her legs. She looks pretty, if probably a bit garish.

MRS. SIEZMAGRAFF. *(To Betty.)* I have these enormous red welts on my upper thighs. It's really unfortunate. I guess if I have sexual relations with Mr. Vanislaw, we better keep the lights off.

Or he could be blindfolded, I guess. I've never done that, but people find it exciting, I'm told. *(Checking what Betty is cooking, or nibbling on something.)* I once saw this movie about a sorority hazing, and they showed these freshmen girls this bowl of wiggling worms, then they blindfolded them and fed them what they assumed was the worms, but it was really just spaghetti, but the girls didn't know that and they choked and vomited and just had a terrible time.

BETTY. A sorority hazing. How unusual.

MRS. SIEZMAGRAFF. Yeah, I guess so. I have no idea what the movie was. I think that was the only scene of it I saw. It seemed to be from the fifties. I think the difference between the innocence of then versus now is that now they'd just go ahead and feed them the worms and not bother about switching to spaghetti. Isn't that sad? I feel something's been lost. But, oh well, we have someone coming to dinner, so I shouldn't let my feelings plummet down to the cellar, should I? La dee dah, oh for the life of a swan. Is that the saying? Oh, for the life of a something.

BETTY. Who is this Mr. Vanislaw?

MRS. SIEZMAGRAFF. Well I found him hiding in the women's changing room. He had a camera and was taking pictures. *(Betty looks alarmed; Mrs. Siezmagraff is happily oblivious.)* He said it was harmless, just for his personal use. Some of the women hit him, but I think, you know, "different strokes for different folks." That's such a good phrase, don't you think? I like men who like women; they're my favorite kind. Oh that Buck here is real cute, don't you think?

BETTY. I think he's an idiot.

MRS. SIEZMAGRAFF. Really? Well, everyone tells me I have bad taste in men. *(Looks out to deck; happy.)* Oh, here comes Mr. Vanislaw now. Yoo hoo, over here! *(Mr. Vanislaw enters. He is over 40. He is wearing a raincoat and nothing else except sneakers. He is maybe unshaven. Very unsavory.)*

MR. VANISLAW. Hi, there, baby, what's hanging? *(With his back to the audience, he opens up his raincoat and exposes himself to Mrs. Siezmagraff. She seems enchanted. Betty screams in horror. Laughter.)*

MRS. SIEZMAGRAFF. Oh, Mr. Vanislaw, you're a card. *(Looks closer, near his genital area.)* What an interesting tattoo. Is that the devil? I love where his pitchfork is pointing, it's very playful.

BETTY. Mrs. Siezmagraff, you've brought a derelict into the house. And a sex maniac.

MR. VANISLAW. Look at my dicky! *(He shakes himself at Betty; we still only see his back.)*

BETTY. Really, I can't permit this. Please close you raincoat.

MRS. SIEZMAGRAFF. Oh, Mr. Vanislaw … not everyone has a sense of humor, so maybe you better keep your raincoat closed, at least for now. Oh, I want you to meet my daughter. She's taking a nap in her room. Why don't you go in there and introduce yourself to her?

MR. VANISLAW. Alright. *(With energy and purpose, Mr. Vanislaw goes into Trudy's room.)*

BETTY. Mrs. Siezmagraff, I must protest. Have you no sense of what's appropriate? *(Terrible screams from Trudy's room. Trudy comes rushing out, hysterical. Mr. Vanislaw follows behind, redoing his raincoat, laughing.)*

MR. VANISLAW. She didn't like my devil tattoo.

TRUDY. Someone broke into my room!

MRS. SIEZMAGRAFF. Trudy, don't exaggerate. No one broke into your room, it wasn't even locked. And this is Mr. Vanislaw, he's our dinner guest.

TRUDY. Are you insane?

MRS. SIEZMAGRAFF. Why do people ask me that all the time? It's so rude. No, I'm not insane. Do I seem insane to you? And if I was insane, would I necessarily know it? I doubt it. So it's really a meaningless question. Mr. Vanislaw, do you think I'm insane?

MR. VANISLAW. Where's the person with the head in the box?

MRS. SIEZMAGRAFF. Well, now, we don't know that there's a head in the box. It could just be hats.

MR. VANISLAW. Where is he, where is he? *(Laughter. Mr. Vanislaw briefly notices the laughter, but then focuses on trying to find the room of the person he's been told about. However, he manages to go into all the wrong rooms.)*

MRS. SIEZMAGRAFF. Now don't you go molesting him. Unlike my daughter, he's a boy, and it's not nice for a gentleman to molest a boy.

TRUDY. I don't understand. And it is alright for a man to molest a girl?

MRS. SIEZMAGRAFF. Well, it's certainly more normal, I'm sure you'll grant me that.

MR. VANISLAW. *(At Betty's room.)* Is this his room?

MRS. SIEZMAGRAFF. No, no, it's over there. *(Mrs. Siezmagraff points to Keith's room.)*

MR. VANISLAW. *(Opening the door, happy, playful.)* Helloooooo -ooooo there, I've come to get you. *(Mr, Vanislaw lets himself into Keith's room. Long silence. Everyone listens.)*

MRS. SIEZMAGRAFF. Well, they seem to be getting along fine.

TRUDY. Mother, why did you bring this person back to dinner?

MRS. SIEZMAGRAFF. Well, for company for me. Your father's dead. I need some male companionship. *(Knocks on Keith's door.)* Don't you be too long in there, Mr. Vanislaw. You're my guest, don't forget. *(To Betty and Trudy.)* I'm not quite sure why everyone finds Keith so fascinating.

TRUDY. Well, he's sensitive and withdrawn. Sensible women like that.

BETTY. I wonder if we should call the police about Keith.

MRS. SIEZMAGRAFF. I don't think so. He might interpret that wrong. *(Knocks on Keith's door.)* I hope you're not dismembering bodies or anything in there. *(Laughter.)*

BETTY. *(Annoyed at the laughter.)* In what way is that funny?

VOICES. We're uncomfortable. And so we laughed. We didn't know what else to do.

BETTY. Oh. Odd.

MRS. SIEZMAGRAFF. Did anyone else just hear voices from the ceiling?

BETTY. It's the people who've been laughing. They seem to be talking from time to time now.

MRS. SIEZMAGRAFF. Oh. Well, if I'm the only one hearing it, maybe it's a reaction to being stung by the sting ray.

BETTY. But you're not the only one hearing it.

MRS. SIEZMAGRAFF. Well, no one else seemed to hear it.

TRUDY. Mother, we all heard it.

MRS. SIEZMAGRAFF. Well, you're not a very reliable witness, Trudy. After all, you said your father forced you to have sex with him.

TRUDY. He did.

MRS. SIEZMAGRAFF. Well, that's not what he told me. He said

you seduced him.

TRUDY. Mother, I was underage.

MRS. SIEZMAGRAFF. It's never too young to be a flirt. Flirting with your father ... it's disgusting. Why do you insist on being so competitive with me?

TRUDY. My therapist says I shouldn't even talk to you. And that it's impossible to debate anything with you because you're insane and you're sick.

MRS. SIEZMAGRAFF. Betty, do you talk to your mother this way?

BETTY. No. But I wasn't molested by my father.

MRS. SIEZMAGRAFF. Well, neither was Trudy.

TRUDY. I was too.

MRS. SIEZMAGRAFF. Was not!

TRUDY. Was too!

MRS. SIEZMAGRAFF. Was not! *(Laughter. To laughter; irritated.)* Why is that funny?

VOICES. You were arguing about something very serious in a childish way, and it made us laugh.

MRS. SIEZMAGRAFF. Well, you're just a bunch of insensitive boobs, that's all I can say. *(Enter Buck.)*

BUCK. Someone say something about boobs?

MRS. SIEZMAGRAFF. Oh hello, Buck. Aren't you attractive this evening? Tell me, you find me more attractive than my daughter Trudy, don't you?

TRUDY. Mother! *(Trudy storms off to her room.)*

MRS. SIEZMAGRAFF. Trudy always overreacts to everything. *(To Buck.)* And she's not good at putting out. While I am. We can keep the lights off so you don't see the welts from the sting ray.

BUCK. Cool.

BETTY. Mrs. Siezmagraff, I'm shocked!

MRS. SIEZMAGRAFF. Well, my husband's dead, my daughter is rude to me, and God knows when Mr. Vanislaw is coming out of that room with Keith. So what else do you expect me to do?

BETTY. I expect you to eat dinner and make pleasant conversation.

MRS. SIEZMAGRAFF. We'll microwave the dinner up later. Come on, Buck. Let me show you some tricks I learned when I visited my husband in prison.

BUCK. Cool. *(Buck and Mrs. Siezmagraff go off to Mrs. Siezmagraff's room. Betty looks around the room.)*

BETTY. But I've worked so hard on dinner.

VOICES. *(In sympathy.)* Awwwwwwwwwww ... *(Betty looks startled at their sound. Not sure she likes getting sympathy from them. Looks confused. End scene.)*

Scene 4

After dinner. Everyone is playing charades: Mrs. Siezmagraff, Buck, Trudy, Betty.

Keith is also present, but uncomfortable to be in a large group and unhappy to be part of a game. He has his arms wrapped around himself. He mostly just watches what happens, but otherwise tries not to interact much.

Betty is in the midst of her turn, which has been going on for a while. She is presently acting out a sneeze, but pulls on her ear to signal that it's a "sounds like" clue.

TRUDY. Sneeze!!?

MRS. SIEZMAGRAFF. No, sounds like sneeze. Knees?

BUCK. Keys?

MRS. SIEZMAGRAFF. Fleas. March something fleas. *(Betty shakes her head "no.")*

TRUDY. Not fleas.

BUCK. Sleaze! *(Betty shakes her head "no.")* Not sleaze.

MRS. SIEZMAGRAFF. Rhymes with sneeze. Everything rhymes with sneeze. I'm sick of this word. Go back to the fifth word again. *(Betty holds up five fingers for the fifth word. Then taps her forearm with one finger, meaning first syllable.)*

TRUDY. Sssssh, fifth word again. First syllable. *(Betty acts "cold" — shivering, etc.)*

MRS. SIEZMAGRAFF. Cold. Freezing.

BUCK. Fucking cold.

TRUDY. Shiver. Shiver me timbers.

MRS. SIEZMAGRAFF. March of the something Shiver. Shiva. *(Betty shakes her head. Changes her "cold" routine to acting like she's getting sudden chills, so she will be still, then will shudder suddenly.)* Shock treatments. *(Betty shakes her head. Does a sudden cold chill again.)*

TRUDY. Sudden chills! *(Betty nods enthusiastically, points to Trudy.)* Sudden chills. Chills. March of the Something Chills.

BUCK. March of the Big Chills. That movie was cool.

TRUDY. March of the Chill. March of the Children. "March of the Siamese Children"!

BETTY. Yes! Finally!

TRUDY. Hooray!

BUCK. What's "March of the Siamese Children"?

TRUDY. Didn't you ever see *The King and I*?

BUCK. What? Shakespeare?

MRS. SIEZMAGRAFF. Maybe we should have a time limit. That took half an hour to get.

BETTY. I thought it would never end.

TRUDY. You did very well.

MRS. SIEZMAGRAFF. Whose turn is it — Keith's? *(Keith looks horrified, makes whimpering sounds.)* Well, your turn is soon, Keith. But maybe Mr. Vanislaw can go next. Where is Mr. Vanislaw?

TRUDY. Mother, he's in the bathroom in Buck's room. Let's just leave him there.

MRS. SIEZMAGRAFF. Well, what's he doing there for half an hour? *(Crosses toward Buck's room; calling out.)* Mr. Vanislaw, we miss you. It's your turn. Are you going to come out soon? *(Exits into Buck's room.)*

TRUDY. I think something's wrong with Mr. Vanislaw.

BUCK. I think he's funny. He's a coot

TRUDY. Well, Keith doesn't seem to like him. Keith, you didn't like Mr. Vanislaw, did you? *(Keith looks up at her and shakes his head "no.")* What did the two of you do in there for so long? *(Keith shrugs. Laughter.)* What was funny, I don't understand.

23

GROUP OF VOICES. We were thinking of something else. *(Keith looks startled. He's never heard the Voices speak before. The others are blasé about it by now.)*

TRUDY. Well, please pay attention to us if you're going to laugh please.

BUCK. God, this is a weird house. *(Enter Mrs. Siezmagraff, dragging Mr. Vanislaw by the hand.)*

MRS. SIEZMAGRAFF. Someone's going to have to mop up in there after Mr. Vanislaw. I don't know what the hell he was doing. *(Laughter.)*

TRUDY. Mother, why can't you have normal friends?

MRS. SIEZMAGRAFF. Well, why can't I have a normal daughter. Okay, where's a piece of paper for Mr. Vanislaw? *(Betty offers Mrs. Siezmagraff the bowl with papers with charades titles in them. Mrs. Siezmagraff reaches in and hands Mr. Vanislaw a piece of paper.)* Now can you read, or are you on drugs?

MR. VANISLAW. I can read. It says ...

MRS. SIEZMAGRAFF. No, don't tell us. Make us say the word by silent clues. This is charades. Remember, we explained it to you before you went to the bathroom. Remember, Buck acted out "Nutcracker Suite."

MR. VANISLAW. *(Likes the word.)* Nuts. *(Starts to undo his coat.)*

MRS. SIEZMAGRAFF. That's right, nuts. Now keep your raincoat closed, Mr. Vanislaw. Betty and Trudy have made a special request.

MR. VANISLAW. They're very controlling.

MRS. SIEZMAGRAFF. Yes, they are. Keith, are you paying attention? Mr. Vanislaw is about to give clues. *(Keith hunches up and looks frightened, looks away.)* Well, listen closely then, Keith. If you have any ideas, just call them out. Okay, we'll start now. Mr. Vanislaw, begin now. *(Mr. Vanislaw laughs energetically, then holds up one finger, hoping someone will say "one.")* Wait, wait, tell us what we're going for. Is this a song title, or a title of a book, or a movie title, or what? *(Mr. Vanislaw looks at the paper, then shrugs, not knowing.)* Well, fine, so we're going for something, but we don't know what. Okay, that's fine.

TRUDY. Why does he have to have a turn? He's a derelict.

MRS. SIEZMAGRAFF. Darling, don't you use that word, it's

24

rude to Mr. Vanislaw. Go ahead, Mr. Vanislaw. *(Mr. Vanislaw holds up index finger, for the word "one.")* First word. *(Mr. Vanislaw continues to hold up index finger.)* Yes, we got it. This is the first word. Now give us a clue.

MR. VANISLAW. This is a clue. What I'm doing.

MRS. SIEZMAGRAFF. Oh.

BUCK. Finger.

MR. VANISLAW. No, not finger.

MRS. SIEZMAGRAFF. Don't speak, just shake you head. *(Mr. Vanislaw shakes his head "no.")* First word. Not finger. Index finger. Index. Index of Forbidden Books. *(Mr. Vanislaw shakes his head "no.")*

BETTY. One. Is it the number one?

MR. VANISLAW. Yes!

MRS. SIEZMAGRAFF. Mr. Vanislaw, no talking. Just nod yes or no please. *(Mr. Vanislaw nods "yes" energetically. Then he starts taking his finger and "touching" his arm, to communicate the word "touch.")* What is this, the second word? Say second word.

MR. VANISLAW. Second word.

MRS. SIEZMAGRAFF. No, don't say it. Hold up two fingers for second word. *(Annoyed, Mr. Vanislaw holds up two fingers.)* Second word. Alright. Now give us the clue. *(Mr. Vanislaw again gives the "touching" clue.)*

BUCK. Arm.

BETTY. Wrist. *(Mr. Vanislaw shakes his head "no.")*

MRS. SIEZMAGRAFF. Skin? Well, what are you doing? You keep touching your arm. Is it arm? *(Mr. Vanislaw nods energetically and points at Mrs. Siezmagraff because she said "touch.")* It is arm? *(Annoyed, Mr. Vanislaw shakes his head "no.")* Well, you nodded yes.

BETTY. *(Trying hard in order to get the game to end.)* Touching your arm. *(Mr. Vanislaw points to her, nods "yes.")* Touching. Touch?

MRS. SIEZMAGRAFF. One touch.

BUCK. One touch banking? *(Mr. Vanislaw shakes his head. Pulls his ear for a "sounds like.")*

MRS. SIEZMAGRAFF. Sounds like. Very good. Is this the third word? *(Mr. Vanislaw nods his head. Does "sounds like" gesture again. Then with his back to audience, he opens his raincoat and points to his genitals. Betty and Trudy are horrified. Keith just stares. Buck laughs. Mrs. Siezmagraff is annoyed. Laughter. Applause.)* Mr. Vanislaw, we told you, no more flashing at people. We're playing a game now. There's a time for everything, and this isn't the time now.

TRUDY. Get him out of here!

MRS. SIEZMAGRAFF. Oh, Trudy, you're such a withered prune. *(Mr. Vanislaw keeps pointing to his genitals, going up to people and pointing.)* Yes. We see it. Thank you. Now put it away. We're playing a game.

MR. VANISLAW. I know we're playing a game! This is a clue. Sounds like what I'm pointing at.

MRS. SIEZMAGRAFF. Oh. Well, that's alright, then, I guess. Girls, it's a clue, he's not being inappropriate now, after all.

BUCK. One Touch Dick.

MRS. SIEZMAGRAFF. No, sounds like, so it couldn't be dick. One Touch Mick. Pick. Lick. Sick.

BETTY. *One Touch of Venus.*

MRS. SIEZMAGRAFF. What?

BETTY. The clue is penis. *One Touch of Venus.*

MR. VANISLAW. Yes!! *(Mr. Vanislaw is delighted, and starts to dance around happily, still with back to the audience and with his coat undone.)*

BUCK. What's *One Touch of Venus.* A porno flick?

BETTY. Well, in Mr. Vanislaw's version, I'm sure it is. Please close your coat now, Mr. Vanislaw, we guessed your title. *(Mr. Vanislaw's victory dance is becoming less a dance and more just his shaking his member upstage. Keith has a very clear view of Mr. Vanislaw's gyrations. Keith is initially embarrassed, and looks away. But then he keeps looking back up, and soon he starts to smile a bit and enjoy Mr. Vanislaw's shaking of his genitals. The other characters are presently not paying much attention to Mr. Vanislaw.)*

MRS. SIEZMAGRAFF. *(To Betty.)* Well. He did very well, then, didn't he? He got that much faster than you got "March of the Siamese Children," I must say.

BETTY. This is the stupidest game of charades I've ever played. Let's call it quits. I want to do the dishes.

MRS. SIEZMAGRAFF. No, no you made the dinner, I think Trudy should do the dishes.

26

TRUDY. Mother! *(Mrs. Siezmagraff suddenly sees Mr. Vanislaw still shaking himself.)*

MRS. SIEZMAGRAFF. Mr. Vanislaw!!!! Close you coat now. *(Mr. Vanislaw finally closes his coat. Keith stops smiling and looks slightly "caught.")* We've all gotten the "penis" clue, it's time to move on to other things now. *(Everyone calms down. Mrs. Siezmagraff and Mr. Vanislaw sit down for a moment.)* Keith, you're awfully silent, do you have nothing to say?

KEITH. I was abused as a child. The memories are starting to come back to me. I think that's why I cut people's heads off. *(No one moves. He gets up and goes to his room. Silence. Everyone is blank faced.)*

MRS. SIEZMAGRAFF. Well, who's going to do the dishes?

BUCK. I'll do 'em. Maybe you and Mr. Vanislaw want to take a walk by the ocean.

MRS. SIEZMAGRAFF. What a lovely idea, thank you, Buck. Mr. Vanislaw, you want to take a lovely walk. By the beach?

MR. VANISLAW. I can air my penis.

MRS. SIEZMAGRAFF. Well, yes, if it needs airing. *(Laughs.)* My, you're quite a handful. Trudy, dear, don't wait up. Who knows when we'll be back. *(Mrs. Siezmagraff and Mr. Vanislaw exit merrily out to the deck and the beach beyond.)*

BUCK. I'm horny. I'm gonna go to a singles bar and pick up some chicks.

BETTY. I thought you were going to do the dishes.

BUCK. No. You do 'em. I gotta get laid. Catch ya later. *(Buck exits. Betty and Trudy sit in silence for a second. They look pleasantly at one another. Betty and Trudy feel something vaguely unpleasant has happened, but they can't presently remember what it was. After a bit.)*

VOICES. What did Keith say?

BETTY. What?

VOICES. Did he say … he cut off heads?

BETTY. I think so. Trudy, did you hear him say he cut off heads?

TRUDY. He said he was an abused child. I was an abused child too. I want to comfort him. *(Goes to his door.)* Keith, are you alright? Can I come in?

KEITH. *(Off.)* I'm busy now. Leave me alone please.

TRUDY. He's so hard to have a relationship with.

BETTY. Trudy. He said he cut off heads. *(Laughter. To ceiling.)* I don't think that's funny.

VOICES. No, you're right. It's not funny. Sorry.

BETTY. Should we call the police?

TRUDY. No. Betty, he's in pain. Psychological pain.

BETTY. I don't know. I don't feel that sorry for him if he's cutting people's heads off.

TRUDY. Well, he probably has an irresistible urge.

BETTY. Mmmm. I suppose.

TRUDY. *(Knocking on Keith's door.)* Were you abused very badly, Keith? I'd love to hear about it. I mean, if you'd like to share it with someone.

KEITH. *(Off.)* I don't like to talk about it. I'm sorry I brought it up.

TRUDY. Well, it's not good to keep your emotions in, Keith.

KEITH. *(Off.)* Please, I'm fine.

TRUDY. Keith, I want to comfort you. *(Keith opens his door.)*

KEITH. I know you're being nice, but I can't be around people for too much of a time, and that charades game your mother forced me to be around went on for hours. So please, let me be by myself.

TRUDY. Well, what are you doing in there all that time?

KEITH. Nothing. I'm playing with my collection.

TRUDY. What collection?

KEITH. Just various things I've collected.

BETTY. *(Polite but worried.)* Keith, what have you collected? Do you have body parts in your room?

KEITH. Well, I have two feet.

BETTY. Oh my God.

KEITH. I have two feet. On the end of my legs. They're standing inside the door, so I have two feet inside my room. *(Enjoys his joke.)*

BETTY. Oh. Well, what's in your hatbox?

KEITH. Hats! Look, I can't talk any more, I'm sorry, I have seizures if I talk to people for too long. You don't want me to have a seizure, do you?

BETTY. No. I guess not.

TRUDY. Well, if ever you want to talk, I'm here, Keith, okay?

KEITH. Yeah, yeah, yeah. Where's Mr. Vanislaw?

TRUDY. He's taking a walk with my mother.

KEITH. Well, if you see him, tell him he can come in my room

28

later. *(Keith closes the door.)*

TRUDY. How could he possibly like Mr. Vanislaw???

BETTY. Well ... I think he's crazy.

TRUDY. Who? Mr. Vanislaw?

BETTY. Well, he's crazy too. But I think Keith is crazy. This summer share isn't turning out at all as I imagined.

TRUDY. Really? I sort of imagined it this way.

BETTY. You did?

TRUDY. Well, my mother always does something to cause trouble. I'm going to take some pills and go to sleep. Good night. *(Trudy exits to her room. Laughter.)*

VOICES. That was so abrupt!

BETTY. Yes, it was abrupt. Well, I guess I should do the dishes. Although I did cook the dinner. But then no one else will do them if I don't.

VOICES. Don't do them if you don't want to.

BETTY. Well, I suppose I could go for a walk.

VOICES. That's a good idea. Go for a walk.

BETTY. Alright. I will. See you later. *(Betty leaves. Applause. Laughter. Sigh. Pause. Silence.)*

VOICES.

Nothing's happening right now.

(Silence.)

I'm getting bored.

Keith — do you want to come out and entertain us for a while? Keith?

Well, he's hopeless.

Gosh, we're just staring at the furniture.

We're just staring.

(Calling plaintively.)

Somebody ... Somebody ...

(Lights go out. End scene.)

Scene 5

The same, later. The house is dark.

Mrs. Siezmagraff and Mr. Vanislaw come stumbling in.

MRS. SIEZMAGRAFF. Sssssshhh! You'll wake everyone. *(Turns on the lights.)*
MR. VANISLAW. I turn into a werewolf at 3 AM.
MRS. SIEZMAGRAFF. Really. You know, I think I had too many margaritas. I think I have to lie down right away.
MR. VANISLAW. You feel lightheaded? Do some jumping jacks.
MRS. SIEZMAGRAFF. No, Mr. Vanislaw, I need to rest just a moment. Oh dear. Excuse me, I just need to lie down. *(Mrs. Siezmagraff lies down on the floor, passes out. Mr. Vanislaw looks at her.)*
MR. VANISLAW. Stupid cow. Can't hold her liquor. *(Keith looks out of his room.)*
KEITH. Pssssss.
MR. VANISLAW. What is that?
KEITH. Psssssss.
MR. VANISLAW. Someone pissing?
KEITH. *(Shyly, kind of sweet.)* Mr. Vanislaw ... I'm awake if you want to come visit for a while.
MR. VANISLAW. No, I want a woman now. *(Kicks the body of Mrs. Siezmagraff.)* Wake up, cow. Uh, she's a drunk. She can't stay awake after seven margaritas. I can drink lighter fluid and it doesn't affect me. *(Laughter.)*
KEITH. Would you like to see more of my collection?
MR. VANISLAW. Which room is Betty in?
KEITH. Betty doesn't like you.
MR. VANISLAW. That's alright. I enjoy struggle. Which room is she in?
KEITH. I don't want to say.
MR. VANISLAW. Oh, go to bed, little boy, you're annoying.

30

Betty, Betty! *(Mr. Vanislaw goes off to Betty's room. Keith watches after him, disappointed; then goes back into his room, closes the door. A second later Mr. Vanislaw comes out.)*
MR. VANISLAW. She's not there. Where is the cow woman's daughter? Oh, Trudy ... Mr. Vanislaw is here. *(Mr. Vanislaw goes into Trudy's room. Inside the room, she screams. Keith pokes his head out of his door. Vocal sounds of struggle inside Trudy's room.)*
KEITH. Trudy, are you alright?
TRUDY. *(Off.)* Stop it! Help! Help!
KEITH. Trudy, should I get your mother? *(Trudy's struggle continues, but her sounds are more muffled now. Keith goes over to Mrs. Siezmagraff.)* Mrs. Siezmagraff. Mrs. Siezmagraff. Can you wake up? It's your daughter. I think something is happening to her. Mrs. Siezmagraff.
MRS. SIEZMAGRAFF. *(Stirring.)* Hello. Come in please. Oh my head. Good Lord.
KEITH. Mrs. Siezmagraff. I think Trudy needs you.
MRS. SIEZMAGRAFF. Oh, that child. What is it this time?
KEITH. I think Mr. Vanislaw is raping her.
MRS. SIEZMAGRAFF. Did Trudy tell you that? That girl thinks men are lusting after her continually, and between you and me, they're not.
KEITH. *(Emphatic, trying to get through.)* I think he's raping her now.
MRS. SIEZMAGRAFF. Well, where is he? I don't even see him.
KEITH. He's in her room.
MRS. SIEZMAGRAFF. Oh, for God's sake! Every time I get a husband or a boyfriend, Trudy's always after them. *(To Trudy's door.)* I hope you're not boring Mr. Vanislaw, Trudy.
MR. VANISLAW. *(Off.)* She's not!
KEITH. Mrs. Siezmagraff ... you're not getting it. Mr. Vanislaw is taking Trudy against her will. Should we do something???
MRS. SIEZMAGRAFF. Do something. Um. Yes, we should. *(Knocks on door.)* Mr. Vanislaw, I think you should come out now. Trudy needs her sleep. Come on out, both of you.
MR. VANISLAW. *(Off.)* I'm almost finished!
MRS. SIEZMAGRAFF. Now, I'm not kidding you two. *(Mr. Vanislaw starts to make orgasm sounds. Mrs. Siezmagraff looks*

appalled.) Goodness. Well, now I'm getting annoyed. *(Knocks on door.)* Stop that in there! *(Mr. Vanislaw comes to the door, doing up his raincoat.)*

MR. VANISLAW. What, what? I thought you were passed out.

MRS. SIEZMAGRAFF. Keith woke me.

MR. VANISLAW. So now you're awake, what do you want?

MRS. SIEZMAGRAFF. Well, I hope you weren't forcing yourself on Trudy.

MR. VANISLAW. Every woman likes me. No need for forcing. I need a nap. Where can I sleep?

MRS. SIEZMAGRAFF. *(Flirtatious.)* Well, Mr. Vanislaw, I assumed you were going to stay with me.

MR. VANISLAW. I need rest. I can't have you groping me all night.

KEITH. You can sleep in my room.

MR. VANISLAW. I'll rest in the boy's room. I like the things in his room. Good night, see you in the morning. *(Mr. Vanislaw goes off into Keith's room. Mrs. Siezmagraff looks depressed and disappointed. Keith is momentarily thinking of Trudy again.)*

MRS. SIEZMAGRAFF. Oh, Lord, this evening is turning out terribly. *(Pauses; to the ceiling.)* I thought I'd hear laughter after that.

VOICES. We're very disturbed. We're not sure we feel like laughter.

MRS. SIEZMAGRAFF. Well, me neither.

KEITH. I hope Trudy is alright.

MRS. SIEZMAGRAFF. Well, she's been through worse things. I'm sure she's fine.

KEITH. *(Nods; starts to think of having God knows what fun in his room; happy.)* Well, good night. *(Keith goes off to his room. Mrs. Siezmagraff at rest for a moment, blank. Suddenly feels guilty about what Trudy's been through. Creeps up to her door.)*

MRS. SIEZMAGRAFF. *(Outside Trudy's door; knocks lightly.)* Trudy, dear, it's mother. Are you alright? Should I come in? Do you want hot cocoa? *(Trudy comes storming out, in T-shirt and shorts or underwear, wrapped in a summer blanket. Mrs. Siezmagraff jumps back, startled.)*

TRUDY. *(Genuinely furious.)* Why didn't you call the police????

MRS. SIEZMAGRAFF. What for?

TRUDY. That horrible man was raping me!

MRS. SIEZMAGRAFF. I hate all this date rape talk.

TRUDY. This was not date rape. You brought a maniac degenerate into the house, and he raped me while you did nothing.

MRS. SIEZMAGRAFF. *(Angry.)* I drank seven margaritas! Do you think I can be expected to be conscious after I drink seven margaritas!!???

TRUDY. Oh, well, in that case, no, just do nothing, it's perfectly understandable. Just like with my father for six years!!!

MRS. SIEZMAGRAFF. Your father is dead, Trudy. Must you insist on speaking against your poor father after he's dead??

TRUDY. I hate you. And I hate my father. And I hate that man. Where is he?

MRS. SIEZMAGRAFF. He's with Keith. And I must say I don't understand what the hell they could be doing. *(Trudy goes to the kitchen, gets a large kitchen knife, and goes off into Keith's room.)* Trudy. Be nice now. *(From inside Keith's room, a terrible scream. From a man's voice. Mrs. Siezmagraff looks quizzical, decides it's probably nothing. Brief pause. Keith comes charging out of his room.)*

KEITH. You better call the police.

MRS. SIEZMAGRAFF. Again? I can't keep calling the police! They'll think I'm a crank. *(Trudy comes stumbling out of the bedroom, carrying something we can't quite see in her upstage hand.)*

TRUDY. *(Hands it to her mother.)* Here. You take it. I don't want it.

MRS. SIEZMAGRAFF. What is it? *(Stares at it; it's vaguely sausage-like, but we don't get a clear view of it.)* I don't understand. What is it?

VOICES. It's his penis, stupid. *(Mrs. Siezmagraff looks horrified. Starts to move toward bedroom, then toward phone, then toward kitchen — an emotional overload of choices, what to do next.)*

MRS. SIEZMAGRAFF. Oh my God. We've got to call an ambulance. Keith, put this on ice. We've got to get doctors to sew this back on.

TRUDY. I don't want doctors to sew this back on. Give it to me, I'll throw it in the ocean. *(Trudy grabs it back from her mother or Keith, and heads toward deck. Mrs. Siezmagraff stops her.)*

MRS. SIEZMAGRAFF. Trudy, if you throw that man's penis in the ocean, we won't be able to find it. How would you like it if

33

someone cut your breast off and threw it in the ocean? Would you like that?

TRUDY. He raped me! *(Trudy shakes the disconnected member at her mother, for emphasis. Perhaps the one and only time we see it clearly. Keith goes back into his bedroom.)*

MRS. SIEZMAGRAFF. Well, even if he did, it wasn't irreparable. I mean, what you've done is a big over-reaction. *(Mrs. Siezmagraff grabs the member back from Trudy and goes toward the refrigerator.)*

TRUDY. Where are you going?

MRS. SIEZMAGRAFF. I'm putting this on ice. *(Opens the freezer door, puts the member in the freezer, closes freezer door.)*

TRUDY. I don't want it in my refrigerator.

MRS. SIEZMAGRAFF. It's not your refrigerator. It's my house. I own it. Now stop acting like a spoiled brat. Oh, I better call an ambulance. *(Picks up phone, speaks into it with intensity.)* Hello. 911? 911?? Is anybody there???

TRUDY. You have to dial, mother. You can't just pick up the phone and expect them to be there.

MRS. SIEZMAGRAFF. I did dial. *(Dials for the first time.)* Hello? Is this 911. There's an emergency here, we need help, a man has lost his penis and I have it in the refrigerator, and I wonder if there's anyone you know of who can sew it back on. *(Listens.)* No, I didn't do it. I'm not a maniac. It was my daughter. *(Listens.)* I don't know if he's conscious. Wait, I'll go see. *(Mrs. Siezmagraff puts the phone down and goes into the bedroom. Trudy stays seated on the couch, sulky and chastised. Pause. Mrs. Siezmagraff screams from offstage. Then comes running out. To Trudy.)* Where is his head? What did you do with his head?

TRUDY. I didn't do anything to his head.

MRS. SIEZMAGRAFF. Well, he's headless. They're going to have to sew back his penis and his head, or else he's going to be totally useless. If we can even find the head. *(Moves back toward the phone.)*

TRUDY. You can't sew a head back on, mother.

MRS. SIEZMAGRAFF. I invite a guest into this house, and this is how he is treated. It's a disgrace. *(Into the phone.)* Forget the whole thing. He's been beheaded. There's no point in re-attaching his penis anymore. *(Hangs up.)* I don't think, anyway. *(Keith comes out of his room. He's not especially bloody, but is now wearing Mr.*

Vanislaw's raincoat.)
KEITH. He hurt Trudy. Trudy's an abused child like me. *(Trudy looks at Keith gratefully, with love.)*
MRS. SIEZMAGRAFF. Abused child. You're both spoiled brats.
TRUDY. Mother, he raped me.
MRS. SIEZMAGRAFF. Well, fine. File a report with the police. But don't cut off his penis. And, you, Keith, I assume it was you who cut off his head. Was that necessary?
KEITH. *(Considers question.)* Necessary? I don't know if it was necessary. Maybe. *(The phone rings. Everyone looks at it. Mrs. Siezmagraff seems horrified, can't imagine why it should ring or who it could be. She goes back to the phone and answers it.)*
MRS. SIEZMAGRAFF. Hello? What? Well, I hung up because he's dead now, I assume. You can't live with your head cut off, can you? Oh, please, do we have to involve the police in it? The people who cut his head off didn't mean to. Well, it was an accident. I don't know how. Here, you speak to them. *(She hands the phone brusquely to Trudy and goes to fix herself a drink from a table or shelf with liquor bottles on it.)*
TRUDY. *(Into phone.)* Hello. What? My name is Trudy. What? Yes, I did. Why? Ummmm ... it was in self-defense. No I didn't cut his head off. Keith did. Well, it was in self-defense too. Uh huh. *(Listens.)* Well, can't we just discuss it in the morning? Now? We have to go to the police station now? Well, it's awfully late. Alright. Alright. *(Hangs up.)* The woman at 911 says we have to go to the police station.
MRS. SIEZMAGRAFF. Trudy, I don't know why you can't leave well enough alone. Come on, let's go, but I hope this won't take all night. *(Trudy gets a coat from her room, or slips into shorts or something. Mrs. Siezmagraff gulps down her drink, and then she, Trudy and Keith leave by the U. door, heading out to the driveway. As they exit, laughter from the ceiling. Mrs. Siezmagraff stares up at it, alarmed as if the house is haunted; and they all three make their exit. Pause. More laughter. Then screams. Then vomiting sounds. Then sounds stop and they speak.)*
VOICES. We feel sick. We wish we were watching *The Waltons*. *(Brief pause. Enter Betty, seeming relaxed.)*
BETTY. Well, I feel much better after my walk.

VOICES. Uh oh.

BETTY. Did you say "uh oh"?

VOICES. No, we didn't say anything. Pay no attention to us. *(Betty looks suspicious. Starts to look around the empty cottage.)*

BETTY. Is anyone here? *(She notices that the door to Keith's room is wide open, which is unusual. Betty goes toward it.)* Keith? *(Betty goes into Keith's room. From offstage, she screams hysterically. She comes running out. Screams some more. Goes to the phone, dials. Forgets how to talk, screams into the phone. Screams again. Then listens.)* What? There's a body. Or part of a body. All bloody. I don't know where its head is. What? You know? What do you mean, you know? *(Listens.)* Oh, someone already spoke to you from here. Uh huh. Alright. Well, what should I do? Just sit tight. Alright. I will. Yes. Thank you. *(Betty hangs up, sits down, sits still, staring straight out. Screams again. And/or cries a bit. Can't seem to figure out how to get through the next minutes.)* Oh God. *(Pause.)* I need a drink. *(Betty goes to the table or shelf where the liquor is, grabs a big bottle of vodka. Pours herself a good stiff drink. Comes back to the couch. Sips her drink. It's awfully strong. And warm. Pause.)* Oh. I need ice cubes. I knew something felt wrong. *(Betty goes to the refrigerator, opens the freezer, looks in, screams hysterically … bolts backward into the room, dropping her glass, falling onto the floor. Laughter. Applause from the ceiling. Blackout.)*

End Act One

ACT TWO

Scene 1

The living room, a short time after previous scene. Betty is on the phone.

BETTY. Mother, it's me. Well not very well actually. No, I'm not married yet. Yes, there are two men here, but I don't think either one of them are likely candidates. Well, I can't say why, mother, but just trust me. *(Listens with irritation.)* Fine, fine ... I'll marry one of them. Do you want me to marry the macho pig or the serial killer? Well, I don't know how much they make a year. *(Listens.)* Mother, I called you because I was upset, but I think I'm going to hang up now. Never mind why I called. Well, there's a headless body in the bedroom and a penis in the refrigerator. *(Pause.)* Mother, are you there? Well, yes the two things are connected. Or rather, they were connected, but Keith or someone cut the body parts off. Well, I don't know why, that's just the sort of thing Keith does, mother. Well, Mrs. Siezmagraff chose him, I didn't. Well, no the other one isn't nicer. On some level I prefer Keith.

VOICES. Get off the phone now, we want another scene.

BETTY. Mother, the voices want me to get off the phone now. The voices. I'm not hearing voices, mother. There are voices. *(Holds phone up toward ceiling.)* Say something.

VOICES. We love to laugh. *(They laugh.)* Ahahahahahahahaha-hahahahahahaha.

BETTY. See? They said they love to laugh. Well, I don't know. Ever since we got here. Mother, they're just a fact, I can't stop them. Uh huh. Uh huh.

VOICES. Get off the phone.

BETTY. I have to go now, mother. I'll probably leave here tomorrow. Uh huh. Uh huh. Well, I'll try to get married, but I have to marry someone specific, don't I? Well, Daddy was specific, wasn't he? He wasn't? He was generic. In what way was Daddy generic? *(Listens.)* Uh huh. Uh huh. This is a longer conversation, mother, and Daddy's not alive to defend himself.

VOICES. How did he die?

BETTY. *(Answering them.)* He died of a heart attack.

VOICES. Oh! *(Laugh merrily.)*

BETTY. *(Looks confused by Voices' response; then to phone.)* No, mother, I didn't laugh. Yes, and I know you know he died, I wasn't talking to you, I was talking to the voices. *(Listens.)* I wasn't in the sun today, mother. Never mind, forget it, goodbye, goodbye. *(Hangs up.)*

VOICES. Entertain us please.

BETTY. What?

VOICES. Entertain us.

BETTY. What should I do?

VOICES. Go to the refrigerator and look at the penis again.

BETTY. I don't want to.

VOICES. Please.

BETTY. No, I don't want to.

VOICES. Pleeeeeeeeeeeeeease.

BETTY. Oh, alright!

VOICES. *(Excited.)* Oooooooooooh!!!

BETTY. *(Going to refrigerator.)* This is so stupid.

VOICES. Open the freezer door. *(Betty opens the freezer door, looks, runs to the sink, and vomits.)*

BETTY. *(Into sink.)* Bllllllllllllllleeeeeeeeeeeehhhhhhhh.

VOICES. *(Pleased.)* Oooooooooooh! Yeah! *(Sound of applause from the Voices. Enter Buck.)*

BUCK. Someone applauding for me?

BETTY. No, it was for me.

BUCK. Oh yeah? What did you do?

BETTY. I threw up.

BUCK. Too much beer, huh? Grody.

BETTY. Yeah.

BUCK. I just balled two chicks on the beach, I think I got jism left for one more. You in the mood?

BETTY. I'm sick.

BUCK. Wanna feel my dick?

VOICES. *(Delighted.)* Ooooooooooh! *(Sound of laughter and applause. Buck looks appreciative.)*

BETTY. *(To Voices.)* Shut up! Shut up!

BUCK. What are you so upset about?

BETTY. Doesn't it bother you, there are all these people in the ceiling?

BUCK. Are they in the ceiling?

BETTY. Or in the air. I don't know where they are. But don't they bother you?

BUCK. No, I like them. They like me. I feel approval.

VOICES. We do like you. We intend to nominate you for a People's Choice Award.

BUCK. *(Very happy.)* Cool. Thanks, guys.

VOICES. Hey, Buck. Why don't you make yourself a drink and put some ice cubes in it?

BUCK. Huh?

VOICES. Make yourself a drink.

BUCK. Okay. *(Buck goes to the refrigerator, gets himself a beer.)* I think I could do with a brew.

VOICES. *(Very disappointed sound.)* Ohhhhhhhhh.

BUCK. What's the matter?

VOICES. We want you to get ice cubes from the freezer.

BUCK. Ice cubes for my beer?

BETTY. *(With a touch of malice.)* Why don't you have a vodka tonic or something?

BUCK. I like beer.

VOICES. She's right. Have a vodka.

BUCK. I don't like vodka.

VOICES. Please, please, please …

BUCK. Alright, alright. *(To Betty.)* You're right, they are kind of annoying. *(Pours himself vodka in a glass.)* Vodka tonic. Vodka's a drink for businessmen. I'm a surfer dude, I like beer. Or tequila with worms in it.

VOICES. Stop complaining. Now get yourself some ice.

BUCK. Okay, okay. *(Buck opens the freezer.)*

VOICES. *(Excited anticipation.)* Ooooooooh. *(Buck, without really looking in, takes ice from the freezer quickly, plops it in his drink, and shuts the freezer door.)*

BUCK. There, I took some ice. Are you happy now?

VOICES. *(Disappointed.)* I guess so.

BUCK. Fuckin' hard-to-figure voices.

VOICES. There's something you didn't see in the freezer.

BUCK. Oh for Christ's sake. *(With irritation he goes back to the freezer. Looks in. Uncertain initially what he sees.)* What is that? *(Sudden realization; screams in horror, slams freezer door shut.)* Bummer! Bummer!

VOICES. Ooooooooo-weeeeeeee! That was fun!

BUCK. Whose is that?

BETTY. Mr. Vanislaw.

BUCK. What is this, some sort of chick revenge thing?

BETTY. I wasn't here when it happened. Do you want to see the headless body in the bedroom? I think that's Mr. Vanislaw too.

BUCK. No, I don't want to see the headless body. What's the matter with you? *(Mrs. Siezmagraff comes back in, with Keith and Trudy.)*

MRS. SIEZMAGRAFF. We're back. And you should have heard the size of the bail we had to put up for these two. It's insane! People are just never presumed innocent in this country anymore.

BETTY. Innocent? There's a headless body in Keith's bedroom, and I found a penis in the refrigerator.

MRS. SIEZMAGRAFF. Yes, yes, we know this. No need to rub it in.

TRUDY. I don't feel well. Any chance I could be committed somewhere?

MRS. SIEZMAGRAFF. Darling, we'll hire you the best lawyers, I'm sure we can get you off.

BUCK. I'd like to get off.

VOICES. Why don't you sleep with Keith?

BUCK. Gross. He's another guy.

KEITH. I want to go to my room.

MRS. SIEZMAGRAFF. You can't go to your room. There's a body in there.

VOICES. We want to see Buck and Keith making out.

BUCK. Well, you're going to have to wait a long time then.

MRS. SIEZMAGRAFF. You know, Buck, if you were in a sub-

40

marine for six months, I bet you'd start to think Keith was looking pretty good.

BUCK. No way, man.

MRS. SIEZMAGRAFF. Yes, way.

BETTY. This is really a side issue, isn't it? And I have a question. Why aren't the police here to remove the body, and look for clues, and all that?

MRS. SIEZMAGRAFF. They said they'd come here first thing tomorrow morning, and we weren't to touch anything.

BETTY. But it's a crime scene. They should be here.

MRS. SIEZMAGRAFF. Darling, this is a summer community, most of the police are in bed at this hour, or off committing adultery with Adelaide Marshall.

BUCK. Who's Adelaide Marshall?

MRS. SIEZMAGRAFF. She's the town randy widow.

BUCK. Cool. Where's the phone book?

MRS. SIEZMAGRAFF. *(Points.)* Over there. *(Buck goes over to the table or shelf where the phone book, and starts paging through the "M's.")*

BETTY. Well, I don't find this appropriate police behavior. If nothing else, they should come and remove the body.

MRS. SIEZMAGRAFF. I told you — they said they'd remove it in the morning.

BUCK. Got it! *(Buck goes to the phone, dials.)*

KEITH. Well, if I can't stay in my room, I need to get some things out of there and put them in another room. And then I need to be able to shut the door. I can't be around people this long.

TRUDY. You can stay in my room, Keith.

KEITH. But you're a girl, it wouldn't be proper. Maybe I should stay in Buck's room, like the voices said.

VOICES. That's a good idea. We'd like to see Keith getting fucked by Buck. We're bored.

BUCK. Be quiet! *(Into phone.)* Hello, Adelaide. This is Buck. Are you there? Pick up if you're there. Well, maybe you're having group sex with the police. But I wanna leave you my number. 555-6822. I'm a real sexy guy, and I think you'd have a good time, baby.

VOICES. Ask her to come over, and then we can watch you, Keith and Adelaide all together. *(Buck hangs up phone.)*

41

TRUDY. Why don't the voices want to watch me have sex?

VOICES. You have a disturbing quality to you. So you don't trigger our erotic imaginations.

TRUDY. And you think Keith isn't disturbing?

VOICES. We find him very disturbing, but he's also strangely sweet. We plan to nominate him for a People's Choice Award. *(Keith is initially pleased and a bit surprised at what the Voices say. Though then he starts to feel uncomfortable as well.)*

KEITH. All this attention is making my head throb.

VOICES. *(Kind of whispered.)* Why don't you kill someone then?

KEITH. That's an idea.

BETTY. Stop, stop! *(Strong, clear-headed.)* The voices are talking too much. It's fine if they want to laugh from time to time — well, it's not fine, but I'm oddly used to it. But enough of this urging sex and murder. We've had enough for one day. Life has to have some dignity too, it's not all disgusting and vicious.

VOICES. She's right. Betty is right. *(They give her a big round of applause. Betty is surprised by their reaction, and also oddly flattered.)* Congratulations, Betty. You have appealed to our higher natures. We are ashamed of how we behaved a few minutes ago. But you are the voice of reason. You are the sort of person for whom *The Waltons* or *Touched by an Angel* is produced and aired. From now on, we will be good people. We love Betty! We send you kisses, Betty. Listen. *(The Voices make non-salacious kissing sounds. Betty is very flattered, smiles, is won over by all the praise.)*

BETTY. Well, thank you very much. *(Pause; feels she's expected to say something else.)* I just feel that people do have aspirations to higher things, to decent living, and I just felt the need to remind everyone of that.

MRS. SIEZMAGRAFF. Yeah, thanks a lot, we enjoyed it.

TRUDY. I feel ashamed. I wish I hadn't cut his penis off.

KEITH. I wish I were a fetus, and hadn't been born yet.

BUCK. I wish I was getting a blow job.

VOICES. Oh, Buck, you're so much fun! Betty, give him a blow job!

BETTY. What???

VOICES. We enjoy how honest Buck is. He's so horny. Why don't you give him a blow job?

BETTY. I thought you wanted to aspire to higher things.

VOICES. She's a prude. Why don't you take her in the other room and rape her, Buck? Rape Keith and Betty both. But videotape it because we want to watch it over and over.

BETTY. I have to leave this house!

MRS. SIEZMAGRAFF. Look, Betty, if you keep over-reacting to every little thing that happens in life, then you're going to grow up just like my worthless daughter Trudy. You've got to learn how to have fun in life. I like to go, go, go! It's like Auntie Mame said — life is a banquet, and most poor suckers are starving to death. But me, I stuff myself at the banquet — I stuff my mouth full of shrimp and chopped liver and pastries and champagne, and I mush it all up and I ram it down my throat because I want to live, live, live! *(The Voices applaud.)*

VOICES. Bravo, Mrs. Siezmagraff. You have the most wisdom. You offer a life-is-fun philosophy that is very life-affirming. We love you, Mrs. Siezmagraff. Auntie Mame, Zorba the Greek, and now Mrs. Siezmagraff. We plan to nominate you for a People's Choice Award. *(Mrs. Siezmagraff is very flattered and pleased with their reaction.)*

TRUDY. I seem to be the only one not nominated for a People's Choice Award.

BETTY. I'm not nominated for a People's Choice Award.

MRS. SIEZMAGRAFF. Well, what should we do next? Canasta? Yahtzee? Strip poker?

TRUDY. I don't want to play strip poker.

KEITH. Neither do I.

MRS. SIEZMAGRAFF. Oh the young people nowadays. Big bores.

VOICES. Oh, the phone's going to ring. *(They all look at the phone. It rings. Mrs. Siezmagraff is impressed. Goes to phone.)*

MRS. SIEZMAGRAFF. Hello? Who is this? Oh. Yes, he is. Hold on. *(Hands phone to Buck.)* It's Adelaide.

BUCK. *(Very happy.)* Hey, doll. How's it hangin'? Yeah? How many men? How big was the biggest one? Baby, I got him beat by a mile.

TRUDY. Well, hardly a mile, I've seen pictures.

KEITH. You have?

BUCK. *(To Trudy and Keith.)* Sssssh! *(Back to phone.)* Yeah. Cool. What's your address. Uh huh. Uh huh. You got it, babe. What? Uh, I doubt it — but I'll ask. *(Away from the phone.)* Hey, Keith, you wanna meet a foxy lady?

KEITH. No, thank you.

BUCK. *(Back into phone.)* Sorry, babe. Well, I'll see if I can pick up any hitchhikers. Cool. Okay, babe. I'm comin' over. And then ... I'm comin'. *(Hangs up.)* Thank God she called back. I have so much testosterone if I don't come twenty times a day my brain gets soggy. See ya later!

VOICES. Don't go, Buck!

BUCK. Sorry, guys, gotta! I'll be back for my shut-eye! *(Buck exits.)*

MRS. SIEZMAGRAFF. Well, I must say, I feel a little offended. We've all been through a trying time tonight, but I feel as a group we should stick together, and not go running off.

TRUDY. Well, you told him about the randy widow, didn't you?

MRS. SIEZMAGRAFF. Oh shut up, Trudy.

KEITH. I have to go to bed now. My head hurts.

MRS. SIEZMAGRAFF. No, let's play a game. Or tell camp stories and roast marshmallows. Betty, you haven't had it that hard today, want to stay up and keep me company, and let the two psychos go to bed?

BETTY. No, thank you, Mrs. Siezmagraff, I don't want to roast marshmallows with you. I, for one, want to go to bed and forget everything about this horrible day; and then when the police come tomorrow, I'm getting a bus schedule and I'm leaving here.

KEITH. I need to lie down somewhere in quiet. Can't I just use my own room? I promise not to cut the body up.

MRS. SIEZMAGRAFF. Oh, do what you want to it, I don't care. I'm in a bad mood suddenly, I need to sleep too. Trudy, go to your room! If you hadn't over-reacted to Mr. Vanislaw, this whole miserable thing wouldn't have happened.

TRUDY. I hate you! I wish you were dead! *(Trudy runs off to her room. Keith starts to go to his room, and stops.)*

KEITH. You know, maybe I should stay in Buck's room tonight. I mean, so I don't do anything with the body.

MRS. SIEZMAGRAFF. *(Temper tantrum.)* I don't care what any

of you people do! The younger generation is lacking in gratitude and _joie de vivre_. Fuck you and all your hat boxes! *(Mrs. Siezmagraff storms off to her room.)*
KEITH. Do you think Buck will be angry if he finds me in his room?
BETTY. I don't know, Keith. I'm going to take a bath. I feel dirty.
VOICES. You look dirty. *(Laugh.)*
BETTY. *(To Voices.)* Fuck you, fuck you, fuck you. *(To herself.)* To hell with my bath, I want to be unconscious right now! *(She exits off to her bedroom, slams the door.)*
KEITH. I've gotta rest. I don't think Buck will mind. *(To Voices.)* Good night. *(Keith exits to Buck's room. Maybe turns the lights out. Nothing happens for a while.)*
VOICES. Well, gosh. I didn't think they were really going to bed. Oh, people! Entertain us please. Time to look in the freezer again. Or just come out and bicker in front of us again, and exchange insults. We love insult comedy. Entertain us, someone! Betty! Betty! Oh, Betty! *(There is quiet for a little bit. Bored; like children wanting to annoy, they do rhythmic nonsense syllables, kind of like saying "blah blah blah" in rhythm.)* La da-da da-da da-da. La da-da da-da da-da. A-wooga! A-wooga! Fuck a duck, fuck a duck! Vomit, vomit. Entertainment Tonight! Tell us what Gwyneth Paltrow is doing right this minute!! Come back, entertain us!!! *(Betty comes tearing out of her bedroom. She is wearing a simple nightgown.)*
BETTY. Shut up!!! I need desperately to sleep. If you don't shut up, I'm going to go sleep on a sand dune. *(Terrible sounds of ripping. A piece of the ceiling rips open — or a piece of the wall. And out of this opening come Three People, all joined together. They are the Voices — or at least three of them — who have crashed through the ceiling. They don't quite look like people — they are an "entity" together, they are joined at the hip by tubing (like from a washing machine). This tubing is flexible and lets them move and stretch away from one another, but they nonetheless stay always connected. Or they might all three be connected to one lower body (wrapped in black stretch fabric, say), with their six feet coming out the bottom. Like a three-headed being. Coming out of the tops or sides of their heads are pieces of tubing with bits of wiring coming out of them, as if they had been living somehow inside the ceiling of the cottage, connected to*

wires and tubing and God knows what else. But they have now ripped themselves out of that situation due to the need to confront the people who have so rudely gone to bed and left them with nothing to watch. On their feet there may be large garbage bags tied as enormous shoes. Though meant to be one "entity," their faces do express their individuality. And there are three faces and three voices, those of a man, a woman, and another man. Voice #1 is male, a bit sensitive, chatty, enthusiastic. Voice #2 is female, articulate, together, sometimes charming. Voice #3 is male, a bit macho, capable of anger and being a bully. And all three of them can get ferocious when they're dissatisfied. Presently they're feeling ferocious. The Voices are the laugh track of the house, but now they have shown up in person. Betty screams when she sees them.)

THE THREE FIGURES. ENTERTAIN US!

BETTY. Help! Mrs. Siezmagraff! *(Due to the noise of the figures crashing through the ceiling, Mrs. Siezmagraff, Trudy and Keith all come charging out of their rooms — and are frightened and confused by what they see. Trudy and Keith are dressed for bed. Mrs. Siezmagraff has not changed clothes yet. Betty or Keith turn the lights back on, so we and they get a better look at them.)*

THE THREE FIGURES. Look in the freezer again! Make us laugh. Gross us out. Tell us the latest news of Gwyneth Paltrow. Show us naked pictures of Brad Pitt! Vomit in the sink! Entertain us! Waaaaa-aaaaaaaaa! *(The Three Figures start to cry — "I Love Lucy"-"Waaaaa" style — at their frustration at not being entertained.)*

TRUDY. Oh my God, what is it?

BETTY. They came from the ceiling.

VOICE 1. *(Male.)* That's a good title. *They Came From the Ceiling.*

BETTY. Who are you?

MRS. SIEZMAGRAFF. Do you play charades?

VOICE 2. *(Female.)* No, thank you. We prefer to watch.

THE THREE FIGURES. ENTERTAIN US!

KEITH. *(Feels he should oblige them; sings shyly.)*
　　Me and my shadow,
　　Strolling down the avenue,
　　Me and my shadow …

BETTY. *(To Keith.)* Stop it! I don't know what's happening.

THE THREE FIGURES. We are so intrigued by the case of the headless body with the penis in the refrigerator. We want this case to go on *Court TV*.

MRS. SIEZMAGRAFF. Oh, what a good idea. And Trudy darling, we'll hire a marvelous attorney who can get you off.

THE THREE FIGURES. We can't wait that long. We want the trial now.

MRS. SIEZMAGRAFF. But it's the middle of the night.

THE THREE FIGURES. Now. Gratify us now.

MRS. SIEZMAGRAFF. They're so demanding.

THE THREE FIGURES. Now, now! *Court TV* now!

MRS. SIEZMAGRAFF. *(Suddenly oddly willing.)* Alright.

BETTY. Wait a minute. Who are these creatures? Are they aliens? Should we call the police?

MRS. SIEZMAGRAFF. We can't keep calling the police every time some little thing happens. I mean, we're used to hearing them laugh all day long, now they've just shown up in person.

THE THREE FIGURES. Mrs. Siezmagraff, you are filled with wisdom. We love you!

MRS. SIEZMAGRAFF. Well, thank you. Now how shall we begin the trial?

BETTY. Well, it won't be binding. There's no judge, no jury, it's not a real trial.

VOICE 3. *(Male; angry, nasty.)* We know that, Betty! But it will be good practice for the real *Court TV* trial. And you'd all gone to bed and we had nothing to look at!

BETTY. Okay, okay. Don't be mad.

VOICE 3. Fucking cunt!

VOICE 2. *(Smiles, charming; she's kind of articulate and pleasant much of the time.)* But we don't want to offend you. We just want a little taste of what the case will be like on *Court TV*.

VOICE 1. *(Chatty, enthusiastic; he's not macho.)* We think it has great potential. We loved the Lorena Bobbit case. We loved both cases, his and hers, and how juries found both of them innocent. In her trial, she seemed very sweet, like when she cut off his penis, she was just pushed too far, and he was abusive and horrible! And then in his case, he seemed falsely accused, she seemed like a real maniac. And so both of them got off, it was very amusing! *(All three of them laugh.*) It was a real exercise in switching your point of view.

VOICE 2. It really held our attention. And we were thrilled when several months later Lorena Bobbit was arrested for beating up her mother! She constantly holds our attention.

VOICE 3. We're angry that Andrew Cunanan died and didn't have a trial on television. We weren't ready for his story to be over. We wanted a few more killings and then a long, disgusting trial. We're angry that Michael Jackson's child molestation case was settled out of court. We wanted it on television. We wanted months and months of humiliating, degrading revelations. We wanted to know if his penis is discolored or not. Is it? Is it?

MRS. SIEZMAGRAFF. I'm sure I don't know.

THE THREE FIGURES. Begin the trial please. *(Loud Court TV-like music starts … pulsating, rhythmic, like the music that introduces the evening news or that introduces repeated news coverage of things with titles like "Crisis in the White House" or "President Under Fire." The Three Figures disengage from any wires that helped them lower themselves into the room, and send the wires back up; and the ceiling closes up. Meanwhile D. of them, Mrs. Siezmagraff confers in whispers with Trudy and Keith on courtroom strategy. Keith seems resistant about something, and Mrs. Siezmagraff hits Keith on the arm or shoulder a number of times. Trudy doesn't like that. Also, at Mrs. Siezmagraff's instructions, Keith and Trudy move furniture around to get ready for the trial: The couch is moved so it is in the best place to be a jury box; and a chair is moved so it can be the witness chair. The music finishes, and The Three Figures sit on the couch.)*

MRS. SIEZMAGRAFF. *(Finishing up any furniture adjustments to set up for the trial.)* I don't know which one of us should be Leslie Abramson. Betty, do you want to be?

BETTY. I don't want anything to do with this.

MRS. SIEZMAGRAFF. Well, it seems to me I'll have to be the defense attorney and defend my darling daughter Trudy, who's been so wronged, and her interesting, disturbed friend Keith, who if one of them has to be punished, I think I'll sacrifice him. *(Keith looks worried, but then goes and sits on the side, out of the way.)* Now. My first witness is Trudy Siezmagraff, accused of malicious assault and removing of genitals. *(Trudy sits in the witness chair. Mrs.*

48

Siezmagraff stands by her.) How do you plead?

TRUDY. He raped me.

MRS. SIEZMAGRAFF. No, no, that's not a plea. Guilty or not guilty.

TRUDY. Guilty.

MRS. SIEZMAGRAFF. No, dear. We never say guilty. We say not guilty.

TRUDY. Well, I did cut his penis off, didn't I?

MRS. SIEZMAGRAFF. Darling, it's not your fault. He was raping you. And that was traumatizing. And you were also raped by your father, and both times your mother didn't help you or aid you, and you just had no choice except to cut his penis off. I mean, you did it as a statement, right?

TRUDY. Yes. It was a statement. *(Looks over and checks to see how the jury/Voices like this tack.)*

MRS. SIEZMAGRAFF. You didn't mean it to be irreparable. You intended that it would be sewn back on. Then it would have been fine, just like with Mr. Bobbit, and he could have even made some pornographic films like Mr. Bobbit. Right?

TRUDY. That's right. I wanted to teach him a lesson, but I knew they could sew his penis back on.

THE THREE FIGURES. We liked that pornographic movie showing John Bobbit having sex. We're angry Tom Cruise doesn't show his penis!

BETTY. You know, if I counted the number of times I have heard the word "penis" used today, I could ... well, I don't know what.

MRS. SIEZMAGRAFF. I'm sorry, are you speaking as the prosecuting attorney, or as Betty?

BETTY. Well, Betty.

MRS. SIEZMAGRAFF. Well, we don't need to hear from Betty right now.

TRUDY. I'm not guilty. It was an impulse. I thought it could be put back on. I'm not responsible because I had a traumatic childhood.

VOICES 1 and 2. Poor Trudy. We feel sorry for her.

VOICE 3. Bitch, cutting off his dick.

VOICE 2. *(Angry, passionate.)* She was raped. She was upset. She took a knife and did what any normal woman would do.

BETTY. I object.

VOICE 2. Well, fuck you!

BETTY. *(Strong, clear-headed again.)* I just have to go on record saying I don't believe you are allowed to do anything you want just because you're upset, or you had a bad childhood. I don't mean to minimize the rape — that is terrible, but there are police and courts and you just don't take justice into your own hands. Look at the lynching of blacks when that was done. Mob rule is a bad thing whether it's done by a group of people, or by one person. Trudy, I know it was awful, but you didn't have a right to do what you did. And, Keith, you really didn't have a right to do what you did. *(To everybody.)* We have to agree not to harm one another. That's one of the basic rules of civilization.

THE THREE FIGURES. *(Genuine; even teary.)* We are so moved. You have spoken eloquently. We will now nominate you for a People's Choice Award, after all. You have once again appealed to our better nature.

BETTY. Well … thank you.

THE THREE FIGURES. *(Harsh, angry.)* Trudy, you have fallen from our favor. Betty has convinced us you are responsible for your actions. We want you to receive the death penalty, and we want to see you executed on television!

VOICE 3. *(Makes electric chair noise.)* Bzzzzzz. Bzzzzzzzzz.

VOICES 1 and 2. Kill her! Kill her! Kill the bitch!

TRUDY. *(Crying, hysterical.)* Oh my God, oh my God.

MRS. SIEZMAGRAFF. *(Annoyed at Betty.)* Oh now look what you've done. *(To Trudy.)* Don't worry, Trudy, momma will save you. *(Mrs. Siezmagraff begins to interrogate Trudy. Her voice doesn't change much from her usual voice, but her manner is more lawyerly. Simple, to the point — like a good no-nonsense lawyer on* Court TV.*)* Trudy, you had a horrible childhood, didn't you?

TRUDY. Yes, I did.

MRS. SIEZMAGRAFF. Your father molested you often, didn't he?

TRUDY. Yes, he did.

MRS. SIEZMAGRAFF. And what of your mother?

TRUDY. She did nothing. When I told her about it, she called me a liar and a seducer.

MRS. SIEZMAGRAFF. I call Mrs. Siezmagraff to the witness stand. *(Calls out, as if she's the bailiff now as well.)* Mrs. Siezmagraff!

50

Mrs. Siezmagraff! Come to the witness stand. *(Speaking as herself.)* Coming! *(As bailiff, running the words together.)* Do you swear to tell the truth, the whole truth and nothing but the truth? *(As herself.)* I do. *(As the lawyer again; she is the defense attorney, interrogating.)* Mrs. Siezmagraff, you are the mother of the accused, are you not? *(As herself.)* Yes I am. *(As defense attorney.)* May I say that you are looking especially lovely this evening? *(As herself; genuinely flattered.)* Oh, thank you.

VOICE 1. Objection!

VOICE 2. Irrelevant!

VOICE 3. Sustained!

MRS. SIEZMAGRAFF. *(Annoyed; but moves on; now as defense attorney.)* Mrs. Siezmagraff, did you know that your husband, Trudy's father, raped her repeatedly in her childhood? *(As herself; angry; her eyes flash.)* Did she tell you that? She's a liar!

THE THREE FIGURES. *(Excited by the drama.)* Ooooooooooh.

TRUDY. Momma, momma.

MRS. SIEZMAGRAFF. *(As herself.)* I have to tell the truth, Trudy. *(As attorney.)* Mrs. Siezmagraff, is it not true that Trudy told you what was happening, and you refused to believe her? *(As herself.)* She never told me. She never told me anything. I was a perfect mother. I don't know why she's telling these lies about me! *(As attorney.)* I call to the stand, Mrs. McGillicutty, your Irish housekeeper. *(As herself; baffled.)* I never had a housekeeper. I don't know who you're talking about. *(As attorney.)* Mrs. McGillicutty, you were in the employ of Mrs. Siezmagraff over there, were you not? *(Now she's the Irish maid, speaking with a very pronounced Irish accent.)* Oh, b'gosh and b'garin, yes, I worked for Mrs. Siezmagraff for many years. *(As herself.)* That's a lie! She's a liar! *(As attorney.)* Be quiet! Mrs. McGillicutty, can you prove to us that you worked for Mrs. Siezmagraff? *(As Irish maid.)* Oh yes, m'lord. Here are my pay stubs for my work for five years. *(As herself.)* Those are forgeries! I've never seen this woman before in my life! *(As Irish maid.)* B'gosh and b'garin, Mrs. Siezmagraff, don't you recognize me? I'm Kathleen. I come all the way from Kilarney to be with your family and mind your little daughter, Trudy. *(As herself; getting hysterical.)* I've never seen you. You're a liar! Listen to her accent. She's not really Irish. *(As Irish maid; offended.)* I am Irish. And I worked for you for five years. Trudy, remembers me, don't you, Trudy?

TRUDY. *(Not quite certain what to say.)* Yeah ... I remember you.

MRS. SIEZMAGRAFF. *(As herself.)* Trudy, you're lying! *(As attorney.)* Don't be afraid of your mother, Trudy. Just tell the court the truth. *(As Irish maid.)* Oh, Trudy. Remember you and I spent many a happy hour. I would read you stories about the leprechauns and the funny mischief they would do. You remember, don't you, Trudy?

TRUDY. Yes, Mrs. McGillicutty.

MRS. SIEZMAGRAFF. *(As attorney.)* Mrs. McGillicutty. Did you ever see Trudy's father molest her? *(As Irish maid.)* Yes, I did. *(As herself.)* She's lying! *(As attorney.)* And do you have any firsthand knowledge that Trudy's mother knew her husband was molesting Trudy? *(As Irish maid.)* Yes, I do. *(As herself; vicious and seething.)* That's not true! She's lying! *(As attorney.)* Mrs. McGillicutty, what is the knowledge you have? *(As Irish maid.)* On April 4th, 1978, Mrs. Siezmagraff said to me, "I know my husband is raping my daughter, but I don't want to say anything to him, because I'm afraid he'd leave me." *(As herself.)* You Irish pig! You liar! *(As Irish maid.)* And when she said that, I happened to be speaking into a tape recorder, making a transcription of my special Irish stew recipe, and so I have a recording of her admission on tape. So don't you be calling me a liar, Mrs. Siezmagraff. I'll take you to court and sue you for slander. *(Mrs. Siezmagraff, caught by the Irish maid's evidence, now has full-fledged hysterics, and rushes center stage. As herself; hysterics.)* It's true! It's true! I knew what was going on. And I didn't stop it. I was afraid I'd lose him. It's my fault Trudy was molested over and over and over, and no wonder she attacked Mr. Vanislaw. And I could've stopped Mr. Vanislaw's raping her, but I was drunk! I had had seven margaritas and I passed out. *(Weeps.)* I'm sorry, Trudy, I'm sorry — I ruined your life.

TRUDY. Momma, momma! *(Weeps.)*

MRS. SIEZMAGRAFF. *(Crescendo: on her knees, out front.)* Don't convict my daughter! It's my fault. I didn't protect her. It's my fault. CONVICT ME, CONVICT ME! *(Collapses to the ground, weeps. Trudy, weeping, embracing her mother. They hold each other and continue to weep. The Three Figures are moved, dab their eyes, make sympathetic sounds.)*

THE THREE FIGURES. *(After a bit.)* We are so moved. *(Dab their eyes some more.)*

MRS. SIEZMAGRAFF. Trudy, Trudy.

TRUDY. Momma. Oh, Momma.

THE THREE FIGURES. We are moved out of our minds. We hereby acquit Trudy of all charges. Beloved Trudy, you are free. Go and live your life. *(The Three Figures beam and smile warmly at Trudy and Mrs. Siezmagraff.)*

TRUDY. Oh, Momma, thank you. At last I have the mother I always wanted. And for everything you did in the past — I forgive you.

MRS. SIEZMAGRAFF. Well, it's about time.

TRUDY. What?

MRS. SIEZMAGRAFF. I'm just saying you took a long time to get to forgiveness. A lot of children would have gotten over it a long time ago and not gone ballistic when some man in a raincoat showed them some attention.

TRUDY. I hate you. *(Moves far away from her mother; furious.)*

MRS. SIEZMAGRAFF. Well your grateful period didn't last very long, did it?

THE THREE FIGURES. Now do Keith's trial.

MRS. SIEZMAGRAFF. Oh, God, I don't have the energy. Betty, can you do it?

BETTY. Ummmm ... I'd rather not.

MRS. SIEZMAGRAFF. Look, I did the first one.

THE THREE FIGURES. Try it, Betty!

BETTY. Okay. *(Mrs. Siezmagraff maybe gets herself a soda, and hangs out with the "jury" for a bit. Betty stands by the witness chair, and Keith crosses to the chair, a bit pleased and excited at the attention he's about to get. He sits in the chair.)* Um ... Keith, you cut the man's head off, right?

KEITH. Yes.

BETTY. And you knew what you were doing when you did that, right?

KEITH. Yes.

BETTY. And you've killed other people too, right?

MRS. SIEZMAGRAFF. No, no, no, stop. This is not how to do a trial. Gosh, it's pointless trying to delegate authority, I always have to do everything myself. *(Betty gives up and walks away. Mrs. Siezmagraff goes over to Keith in the witness chair. Tries to do it fast.)* Keith, you were molested, right? And treated really badly, right?

KEITH. Yes. I was. I was molested by twenty people. *(The Three Figures are suitably and gruesomely impressed.)*

MRS. SIEZMAGRAFF. Well, you had quite a large family, didn't you? Or were some of those people neighbors? Never mind, we don't need to know.

KEITH. We had cousins from the Ozarks living with us. And they had all cross-pollinated.

MRS. SIEZMAGRAFF. Cross-pollinated. Please don't make this too interesting, we have to move through this quickly. So — Keith, you were molested by twenty people, and then you were criticized unrelentingly too, weren't you? "Keith, you're too slow." "Keith, you're stupid." "Keith, you're not man enough." "Keith, you're this, Keith, you're that." Am I right, Keith?

KEITH. Yes. That is right. All twenty members of my family said I was worthless.

THE THREE FIGURES. You are worthless.

KEITH. Yes, like that.

MRS. SIEZMAGRAFF. And Keith, right before you cut off Mr. Vanislaw's head, I bet he had been criticizing you, right?

KEITH. *(Uncertain.)* I'm not sure.

MRS. SIEZMAGRAFF. God, you're stupid. Keith, think harder. I think Mr. Vanislaw criticized you unrelentingly just like the members of your large family did. Is that right? Say yes.

KEITH. Yes, he did.

MRS. SIEZMAGRAFF. And I bet you thought that if he kept criticizing you that your head would explode, is that right, Keith? Say yes.

KEITH. Yes, that's right.

MRS. SIEZMAGRAFF. And so because you literally thought your head would explode, you had to kill Mr. Vanislaw, didn't you? And thus your action was actually in self-defense. Am I correct? Say yes.

KEITH. You're correct. I did it to defend myself.

MRS. SIEZMAGRAFF. You see! He's innocent, he's innocent.

THE THREE FIGURES. We see his pain. We hereby acquit him.

Go and find happiness, beloved Keith. You are free.

KEITH. I'm free. I killed out of self-defense because I thought my head would explode.

MRS. SIEZMAGRAFF. *(A bit tired.)* That's right, Keith.

KEITH. And also because I like to cut heads off. *(Mrs. Siezmagraff and the jury/Three Figures are taken aback by this comment.)*

MRS. SIEZMAGRAFF. You're a difficult client, Keith. We'll just take that last comment as kind of ... a joke, I guess. Was it a joke, Keith?

KEITH. Yes, I have a quiet sense of humor.

MRS. SIEZMAGRAFF. Yes you do. Your actions are loud and noisy, but your humor is quiet. Now can we stop *Court TV* for a while? All this strategy and planning has made my head hurt. I've got to lie down. I think I have some Twinkies in my room, my blood sugar is dropping. Excuse me. I need some sugar, and a nap.

THE THREE FIGURES. Wait! Give us some of your wonderful philosophy again before you leave.

MRS. SIEZMAGRAFF. *(Not really in the mood.)* Oh. Um. Life is great. Live, live, live. Eat food at the banquet ... to life, to life, *l'chaim!* (*Mrs. Siezmagraff stumbles/dances off to her room. Trudy looks at Keith longingly.)*

TRUDY. Keith.

KEITH. Yes?

TRUDY. I love you.

KEITH. I love you too.

THE THREE FIGURES. Ahhhhhhhhh. *(Trudy goes over to Keith and reaches out to touch him.)*

KEITH. *(Recoils in fear.)* Please don't touch me.

THE THREE FIGURES. Uh oh.

TRUDY. Okay. But someday I can touch you, can't I?

KEITH. I don't think so.

TRUDY. Life is so unhappy. I want to go to sleep now.

KEITH. Me too.

BETTY. Me three.

THE THREE FIGURES. NO!

BETTY. We're tired.

TRUDY. Keith, why don't you rest in my room? You don't want to be alone tonight, do you?

KEITH. I like to be alone.

THE THREE FIGURES. Don't go yet please.

TRUDY. Well, Keith, I don't want to be alone. You can sleep on the whole other side of the room. I won't come near you, I promise. But I need company.

THE THREE FIGURES. We need company too.

TRUDY. Please I'm exhausted. Keith, will you come with me?

KEITH. Oh, alright.

THE THREE FIGURES. Don't go.

TRUDY. *(Cranky.)* We're tired! *(Trudy and Keith exit to Trudy's room.)*

THE THREE FIGURES. Well, we're not tired. Don't leave us. Betty, help us focus our minds on something.

VOICE 1. I want to see naked pictures of Brad Pitt.

VOICE 3. I want to see naked pictures of Cameron Diaz.

VOICE 2. I want to see Hugh Grant in bed with a prostitute.

VOICE 1. I want to see Clarence Thomas giving Anita Hill a coke can with pubic hair on it.

VOICE 3. That bitch, she lied!

VOICE 2. She told the truth!

VOICE 1. Clarence Thomas likes movies starring Long Dong Silver.

THE THREE FIGURES. We have that in common. *(Happily listing things they love.)* Sex. Murder. Mayhem. Human Interest Stories About Kittens. Kitty and Jose Menendez Served in a Casserole! *(The Three Figures all look at Betty.)*

BETTY. Well, I do think it's rather late. *(Betty tries to leave the room.)*

THE THREE FIGURES. *(Screaming at her.)* We're not done yet!

BETTY. Now, look! — you've had a sexual assault, a removal of genitals, a beheading, and a simulation of a very dramatic trial. I don't know what else you want from us. *(The Three Figures whisper and confer.)*

THE THREE FIGURES. Do you have any of *The Naked Gun* movies on tape? O.J. Simpson is in them.

BETTY. No, we don't. Now, good night.

VOICE 2. Wait! *(Little girl.)* Tell us a bedtime story, Betty. Please.

THE THREE FIGURES. Please, Betty. Please.

BETTY. Alright. But then you've got to sleep. *(Looking vaguely above her.)* And maybe go back into the ceiling if you can.

THE THREE FIGURES. Soothe us. Soooooothe us. *(The Three Figures sit back down on the couch and kind of cuddle together. They luxuriate in the pleasure of the bedtime story to come.)*

BETTY. Alright. Once upon a time ...

VOICE 2. *(Little girl-ish.)* When?

BETTY. Long ago.

THE THREE FIGURES. *(Sighing, satisfied.)* Long ago.

BETTY. There lived a princess.

VOICE 1. Ooooh, a princess. I want to wear a dress.

VOICE 3. Faggot.

VOICE 1. Butch heterosexual bully!

VOICE 2. Please, please, she's telling us a story. Go on, Betty.

BETTY. I don't know what I'm talking about. Okay, there's this princess. And she has a curse on her.

VOICE 1. Oooooo, menstruation. *(The other two giggle.)*

BETTY. Stop it. That's childish. *(The Three Figures look suitably chastised, and settle back down, like children told they've been bad.)* A witch put a curse on the princess, that she had to find true love before 11 o'clock at night, or else ... well, or else. And then at 10:45 the door bell of the castle rang, and in walked ... seven dwarfs, and a gnome, and a person with a hare lip.

VOICE 2. This is starting to wake me up.

VOICE 1. *(Getting excited by his fantasy.)* And the princess was really Andrew Cunanan in drag. And he killed all seven dwarfs, who were gay.

VOICE 2. And the gnome collects shoes belonging to Marla Maples.

VOICE 3. And the person with a hare lip is an S and M dominatrix who bites Marv Albert on the buttocks.

VOICE 1. And then Frank Gifford has sex with Tonya Harding while Kathie Lee watches.

VOICE 2. *(Terribly happy.)* And Amy Fisher has sex with Joey Buttafucco and Charles Manson and a pig! And they make three TV movies about it!

VOICE 3. And then Buck comes home, and he's still horny, so he rapes Trudy and Keith.

VOICE 1. Or maybe just Keith.

VOICE 2. And then Trudy and Keith do it again.

THE THREE FIGURES. They cut off his penis and behead him!

VOICE 1. That's Entertainment Part Two!

VOICE 3. Oh Buck!

VOICE 2. Buck!

THE THREE FIGURES. Oh, Buck! Buck! Buuuuuuu-uuuuuu-uuck! *(Enter Buck.)*

BUCK. Jeez! That Adelaide was nothing but a cock tease. She never let me come, and now I'm so fuckin' horny my nuts hurt. You ever have your nuts hurt?

THE THREE FIGURES. We have an idea, Buck.

BETTY. No, Buck, go outside again. Hurry. *(To The Three Figures.)* You said you were going to sleep. I'll do a better story. Once upon time ...

VOICE 3. We're sorry you're horny, Buck.

VOICE 1. Why don't you fuck Keith finally? It wouldn't be like you're gay. You're just horny.

VOICE 2. You've only had sex twenty times today.

BETTY. No. Buck, run for your life. Don't stay here.

BUCK. *(To Betty.)* What — ya jealous?

VOICE 1. Fuck Keith.

VOICE 3. It's okay with me, man. It don't mean nuthin'. Treat him like a pussy.

VOICE 2. And tell Trudy she's not attractive enough, and you prefer Keith to her.

BUCK. Well ... I do gotta get my rocks off.

BETTY. *(Annoyed.)* You haven't even seen them before. Don't you want to ask who they are?

BUCK. They're the people in the ceiling, right?

BETTY. *(Disoriented by his acceptance.)* Right.

THE THREE FIGURES. They're in Trudy's room, Buck. They're there together. They're waiting for you. Go take your pleasure, Buck.

BUCK. Yeah. Keith'll probably like it. Thanks, guys. *(Calls out.)* Oh Keith. Trudy. Buck is home.

BETTY. Don't let him in! *(Betty tries to hold Buck back, or to block the door. Buck easily pushes her aside. Keith opens the door.)*

KEITH. Oh, hi, Buck.

BUCK. Keith, my man. You're lookin' mighty good tonight.

KEITH. Oh really? Why don't you come in. Look, Trudy, look who's here.

BETTY. Don't go in there, Buck. *(Buck goes into the room. They shut the door behind him. Betty holds her hands over her ears. The Three Figures listen attentively, excited. After a moment the sounds of terrible screams from Buck. Then more screams. During this, The Three Figures are delighted.)*

THE THREE FIGURES. Ooooooooh! Yeah. Go get 'im. Chop off his dick! Chop off his head! Oooooooooooh. Chop him into hamburger! *(The noises of Buck screaming stop. Mrs. Siezmagraff comes charging out of her room.)*

MRS. SIEZMAGRAFF. What is going on here??? I'm trying to sleep, you selfish children! *(Trudy comes out of the bedroom. She's wiping her bloody hands on a dish towel.)*

TRUDY. Mother. We've done it again.

MRS. SIEZMAGRAFF. Done what again?

TRUDY. You know. What we did earlier.

MRS. SIEZMAGRAFF. I don't understand what you're saying.

TRUDY. *(Trying to explain; she doesn't quite understand what made them do it either.)* Buck came back.

MRS. SIEZMAGRAFF. Oh my God. *(Looks into the room.)* Oh my God.

THE THREE FIGURES. Vomit in the sink! Vomit, vomit! *(Keith, also a bit bloody, comes out of the room and stands next to Trudy.)*

MRS. SIEZMAGRAFF. What kind of behavior is this? Are you two just totally insane?

TRUDY. *(Angry, firm.)* Mother — we had very difficult child-hoods.

MRS. SIEZMAGRAFF. Oh "blah, blah, blah" your childhoods. I got a splinter once when I was three. Do you see me killing people?

KEITH. *(Shouts for the first time.)* That's an idiotic comparison, you cow!

MRS. SIEZMAGRAFF. *(Shocked, but ignores his outburst.)* Look, when I got you two acquitted of the charges, that was rehearsal, you know. That wasn't really *Court TV*. That was practice. I can't get you acquitted if you've gone and done it again!

TRUDY. We weren't on *Court TV*?

MRS. SIEZMAGRAFF. No, Trudy. And no matter how pathetic we make you sound, no jury in their right mind is going to acquit you if you've cut off the penises and heads of two people in one day.

TRUDY. They will acquit us. We'll make them cry.

MRS. SIEZMAGRAFF. I don't think so. Goodness, Buck. He was a very nice person. Women like men who put out, Trudy — but you wouldn't know about that.

KEITH. Shut up, you cow!

MRS. SIEZMAGRAFF. Shut up yourself.

TRUDY. You mean I might go to prison?

MRS. SIEZMAGRAFF. Well, I would think so, Trudy.

TRUDY. *(Pointing to The Three Figures.)* They made us do it.

MRS. SIEZMAGRAFF. You really blame people a lot, don't you, Trudy?

KEITH. Don't you pick on Trudy, you cow, or I'll cut your head off.

MRS. SIEZMAGRAFF. Stop calling me a cow.

KEITH. Cow! Cut your head off!

THE THREE FIGURES. Cut her head off, cut her head off.

BETTY. *(Ferocious.)* STOP IT! NO MORE CUTTING OFF OF HEADS!!!

THE THREE FIGURES. Well ... blow up the house then.

KEITH. That's a good idea. They're gonna give me the electric chair anyway. I'm tired of living.

MRS. SIEZMAGRAFF. *(Trying to stop him.)* Now, Keith ... *(Keith goes over to the kitchen area.)*

KEITH. This is a gas oven, isn't it? *(Betty, unprepared for this, tries to appeal to Keith from time to time, saying "no" and "no, Keith" — but he's quite far gone now.)*

TRUDY. Good idea! Let's kill ourselves and mother, and blow the house up. *(Keith turns on the gas jets. Exaggerated sound of gas escaping.)*

MRS. SIEZMAGRAFF. No, Keith. I own this house. And I get rental income. We don't want to blow it up.

TRUDY. *(To The Three Figures.)* Hold her! *(The Three Figures grab onto Mrs. Siezmagraff and won't let her go.)*

MRS. SIEZMAGRAFF. Oh my God.

THE THREE FIGURES. Stay put, bitch.

MRS. SIEZMAGRAFF. I thought you liked me.

THE THREE FIGURES. We like you dead on toast.

TRUDY. *(Emphatic; kind of happy.)* Mother, it's all your fault. And Daddy's fault. And Keith's twenty relatives' fault. And Oliver Stone's fault for making *Natural Born Killers*. And now we're all going to die.

MRS. SIEZMAGRAFF. No, Trudy. Life is wonderful. It's great fun. Whee, wheee, wheeee!

KEITH. I've got the match ready.

BETTY. Keith, don't strike the match.

KEITH. But I want to.

THE THREE FIGURES. Betty, we allow you to escape. Hurry — run out of the house.

BETTY. But stop this from happening.

THE THREE FIGURES. You have ten seconds, Betty. One, two, three ...

TRUDY. Stay here, Betty, and die with us!

THE THREE FIGURES. ... four, five, six, seven ...

BETTY. No ...

THE THREE FIGURES. ... eight, nine ...

BETTY. Goodbye! *(Betty runs like crazy out of there — the door to the deck and the beach and ocean beyond.)*

VOICE 1. We're ready, Keith.

VOICE 2. Light the match, Keith.

VOICE 3. Blow it to fuckin' smithereens, baby!

TRUDY. *(Closes the door Betty left by; looks at her mother, with an evil look.)* Goodbye — Mrs. Siezmagraff.

KEITH. Here goes. *(Keith lights the match. Terrible flash. Sound of enormous explosions. Blackout.)*

Scene 2

Epilogue.

The beach, moments later. Betty comes running out, in her nightgown.

It's dark on the beach. We hear the sounds of waves, and we hear the sounds of explosions in the background. In the distance, behind the dunes, we see a red and orange glow of the house burning.

Betty is scared and out of breath. She looks back to where the house burning is. Then out front again.

BETTY. *(Speedy, upset; partly to herself, partly to the audience.)* Where am I going to sleep tonight? I don't know why the people in the ceiling let me leave. I don't think I could have saved Mrs. Siezmagraff. I don't feel too guilty about it. I mean, they all seemed really terrible. I feel bad for Trudy, sort of ... but well, I don't know what to think. *(Looks out to the audience; includes them directly now.)* Now, actually, I think I'd like to become a hermit. Or I might become a nun if I could live in a convent in an isolated area with no other people around, and where no one in the convent is allowed to speak ever. I'd like that if it was quiet, and peaceful, and if they didn't care if I believed in God or not. *(Another idea.)* Or maybe I could start my own community where people don't speak. And we'd plant our own food, and we'd watch the birds in the trees. And maybe I'm having a breakdown. *(Holds the sides of her head, as if it might fly apart.)* Or is it a breakthrough? *(Hopeful; another possibility.)* Maybe it's a bad dream I had, and am still having. *(Looks around her.)* But I seem to be on the beach. And the house seems to be smoldering somewhere behind me in the distance. *(Looks behind her; the glow is almost out now; the sound of explosions has stopped; we hear the sound of the ocean.)* Isn't the sound of the ocean wonderful? *(Calming down slightly.)* What is it about it that sounds so wonderful? But it does. It makes me feel good. It makes me feel connected. *(Realizing what she said before was a little off.)* Well, maybe I don't have to join a convent where they don't speak. Maybe that's over-reacting. But it is hard to be around civilization. I don't like people. But there are nice people, though, aren't there? Yes. I'm sure you're very nice — although I'm just trying to ingratiate myself to you so you don't try to cut any of my body parts off. *(Laughs, then cries.)* Now I'm sad. *(Suddenly looks up, scared.)* Now I'm frightened. *(The emotions pass.)* No, now I'm fine. Listen to the ocean. That's why I wanted to come on this vacation, and have a summer share at the beach. I wanted to hear the ocean. But you know I forgot to listen to it the whole time I was with those people. But I'm going to listen to it now. *(Listens; she and the audience hear the sound of the waves; tension leaves Betty's face and body.)* Oh that's lovely. Yes. Ocean, waves, sand. I'm starting to feel better. *(Betty smiles at the audience. Closes her eyes. Continues to relax her body. Sound of the ocean continues. Lights dim.)*

End of Play

PROPERTY LIST

Phone
Suitcases (BETTY, TRUDY)
Shovel, hatbox, suitcase (KEITH)
Weights, six-pack of beer (BUCK)
Towels (TRUDY, BUCK)
Bloody rubber gloves (KEITH)
Photo album (BUCK)
Bags of groceries (BETTY)
Bowl of papers for charades (BETTY)
Summer blanket (TRUDY)
Kitchen knife (TRUDY)
A disconnected member (TRUDY)
Drink (MRS. SIEZMAGRAFF)
Bottle of vodka and glass (BETTY)
Phone book (BUCK)
A soda (MRS. SIEZMAGRAFF)
Bloody dish towel (BUCK)
Match (KEITH)

SOUND EFFECTS

The ocean
Sitcom laughter
Screams
Vomiting sounds
Applause
Phone ringing
Terrible ripping sound
Gas escaping from jets
Enormous explosions

AUTHOR'S NOTES

I like to write notes for actors and directors, telling them some of the things I feel I learned about a particular play during production. I learn, of course, from the production itself; and I also learn from actors' auditions, including sometimes learning where people may be misled by something I've written that needs to be clarified.

Most people seem to like the notes. Some directors bristle occasionally. I don't offer the notes as papal encyclicals, but just as some guidance which I hope helps.

Betty's Summer Vacation is a dark comedy in which some very terrible things happen. I find it funny, and many/most audiences seem to have too. I was a little surprised when in early previews at Playwrights Horizons, some audience members were upset and even offended by my seemingly "making merry" about dark matters.

The play was written, initially somewhat unconsciously, as a reaction to the glut of high profile, gruesome and wildly personal court cases that seemed to capture the nation's consciousness on television — the Menendez brothers killing their parents due to alleged sexual abuse (though was that true or made up?); Lorena Bobbit cutting off her husband's penis in the middle of the night and then throwing it into a field (where, amazingly, it was found and re-attached; I never find penises in fields, or at least not so far); the William Kennedy Smith rape trial, with the accusing victim seen with a big blue dot on her face for days and days on television; the Jeffrey Dahmer horror; going back further, the amazingly gripping and dramatic Clarence Thomas/Anita Hill hearings; the O.J. Simpson trial (which I barely make reference to, since I feel the play can't deal with or take in the deeply painful racial resonances of that case).

I wrote the play before the whole Bill Clinton/Monica Lewinsky soap opera, though that was happening during our rehearsals. Once I came late to rehearsal and explained I had been delayed by watching my favorite TV show, *The Presidency in Crisis* (with music and graphics introducing the news coverage very much as if it was the latest network miniseries — which it was).

So people doing awful and/or very personal things that then get discussed by Cokie Roberts on television has become an overwhelming and exhausting commonplace in our twenty-four-hour-a-day media world.

But I've not written a documentary, I've written a play; and it's a farcical play as well, in which we are not meant to EMPATHIZE with the characters the way one is meant to empathize with Blanche DuBois or Willy Loman; it's more like following the stories of Candide and Cunnegonde in *Candide*, or the characters in a Joe Orton farce, or even the characters in a 1930s screwball comedy (though admittedly a dark one).

Those of you who like the play, I think, already know what I mean. Those of you who don't, or those audience members in the future who are upset by it — well, a) there are differences in taste that I can't solve; and b) some people don't like to mix comedy and seriousness, they want it crystal clear and separated. Part of my humor — as an audience member too — is that I often find matters *simultaneously* funny and serious.

Anyone who's experienced the healing laughter sometimes at a twelve-step meeting will recognize how some deadly serious things frequently make us laugh, both by their extremity, when described a certain way, and also by our now having distance from the upsetting thing.

I tend to feel a distance from most fictional work, especially when it's written in a non-realistic style. The audiences who don't like my work seem to me not to know how to have distance from fictional work. It's an acquired taste, I guess. And if a serious topic per se strikes you as never able to be seen in a distanced, comic way, then you're not likely to feel comfortable with most of my plays.

In my play, Trudy has been incested by her father, and her mother is wildly insensitive about it and denies it vehemently to Trudy and others all the time. I would not laugh at this happening in life (where I know it does happen); I would not laugh at it in a "serious" play written in a tone that asked for empathy (and these kind of sincere works tend to be TV movies now, not plays).

But my play is about a world where people do horrible things, and seem disconnected from them, and babble inappropriately about them. I was kind of thrilled with the laugh that consistently greeted Mrs. Siezmagraff's line, in response to being asked if Trudy is indeed her daughter: "Yes. But we don't talk much because her father incested her when he was drunk, and I never did anything about it because I was codependent."

The blithe-and-chatty way that actress Kristine Nielsen did the line, and the way in which talk shows have made "codependent" a buzz word combined to make the audience laugh. They're not laughing at the existence of incest in the world, or at the suffering of people who've gone through that. They are laughing at the way in which our society has changed from the 1950s "let's not talk about it" rule to the 1990s "let me tell you my most intimate feelings on national TV for hours at a time" media behavior. (Are you a secret transvestite and you now want to tell your wife about it? Well, then, why not go on *The Sally Jessy Raphael Show* and tell your poor wife on national television, while Sally clucks sympathetically and has a therapist standing by to say things like, "You feel upset, don't you?")

As a writer I end up being home in the day a lot, and I probably have seen more daytime talk shows than the general population who works nine to five. And, as those who've seen these shows can tell you, Sally Jessy Raphael and of course Jerry Springer and that grinning-at-the-apocalypse blond lady Jenny Jones have glutted the airways with American citizens who are baffling in their willingness to expose their most intimate shames and secrets on television. I remember the first TV talk show I saw on father-daughter incest was moving and upsetting, and seemed a legitimate attempt at dealing with that topic; a few years later, by the time one flips the channels and goes by the twenty-third show doing that same theme, it's clear that the tragedy has shifted in the media from sincere exploration to salacious entertainment. The Christians and the lions, only psychological now.

So, I hope you see the distinction I'm making between making light of something serious like incest, and making satire of the tabloidization of such topics in our culture.

Having said all that, the topic of acting and directing tone now comes up.

My work seems particularly open to going awry tonally. It needs to be real — that is, it needs to have a *genuine psychological truth* behind it — but if it's too real, it will turn heavy-headed and probably unfunny and also off-putting. (So that I personally find some directing/acting interpretations of my work off-putting; but the audience and critics have no way of knowing what's production tone and what's text, and they assume I intend it the way they see it.)

I'll give an example from a student production of my friend Wendy Wasserstein's of how tone can go off. Wendy and I were fellow playwriting students at the Yale School of Drama, and she had gotten into the School with a witty social comedy called *Any Woman Can't*. In the play there's a line where the main character, after a whole series of romantic misadventures and disappointments, says, "I went to Smith College, I thought my life would be different!" The line is meant to be said wryly, by an intelligent woman who knows that's a joke thing to say; you have to say it with self-awareness, because a smart person can only half-mean that statement.

Wendy's second year there was a student production of that play, and the undergraduate actress who played Ginger meant well but was very heavy-handed in her acting. And when she got to that line, she played it for full tragedy, full of angst, sorrow, despair … it was as if Doris Day had approached *Pillow Talk* like *Medea*. In any case, the actress made the play — or at least the line — seem stupid. You thought, gosh, does the author really think going to Smith should protect her from life's ups and downs? And further, does the author think these disappointments are first-rate tragedies, rather than problems that everyone has in one way or another?

While if you read the play, or saw it in a more appropriately toned production, Wendy's play seemed wry and funny.

Everyone in the production meant well, of course; but plays and tones are delicate things.

Anyway … what, if anything, do I have to say about *Betty's*?

BETTY. Betty is meant to be sympathetic and kind of "normal." I intend for her to be the audience surrogate; we get to check in with her to be reminded of how and to what degree the other characters are off.

She's also polite. Buck is gross, but she doesn't read him the riot act usually; she does her best to be nice and pleasant and to send subtle "no" signals that he just isn't open to reading.

Or when Mrs. Siezmagraff tells of how she met Mr. Vanislaw, Betty has to have the appropriate "Good Lord, that sounds crazy" facial responses to this story. (In one rehearsal, we experimented with Betty not reacting negatively — trying to be "fun" or more open or something — but it was disorienting; it made us wonder what was up with Betty, rather than letting us hear this description of a new character and letting us know that, yes, we're meant to find his description inappropriate sounding.)

Betty has a couple of speeches in Act Two where she gets to express her strong opinion about the Voices and about Trudy and Keith's behavior. (The one speech ends with "Life has to have some dignity too, it's not all disgusting and vicious"; and the other one ends with "We have to agree not to harm one another. That's one of the

71

basic rules of civilization.") I intend for these speeches to be sincere, and I hope even stirring.

In talking with the director, Nicholas Martin, before rehearsals, I used to say these Betty speeches should be done the way Jean Simmons would sometimes do a strong "telling the truth" speech in one of her movies — like telling off the emperor at the end of *The Robe*, or finally confronting her psychologically devious family in *Home Before Dark*, or the intelligent gravity she brought to her roles in *Androcles and the Lion*, *Spartacus* or *Until They Sail*.

I'm afraid my Jean Simmons example, though, shows my age and my film buff-dom; and not enough people know what I mean by saying these speeches should be done like Jean Simmons.

More recent movie examples could be the actresses Susan Sarandon or Sigourney Weaver — there's no specific movie I can point to for a "truth telling" speech; but both actresses have an unadorned directness and strength, and you often feel "they're right!" and it's pleasurable to be in their company as they stand up for what they believe in or think.

So it's that kind of sound I'd like for those speeches; I'd like it to be a relief to hear something sensible, balanced and truthful being said in the midst of the play's craziness. (Our original Betty, Kellie Overbey, girlish but strong and intelligent, did a terrific job with the speeches. I'll mention the production more at the end of the notes.)

So Note 1 was — Betty is normal, likeable and a satisfying truthteller. She reacts to the craziness around her, though often tries to be polite. Much of her part is in how she listens and reacts.

TRUDY AND KEITH. Note 2 — Trudy and Keith should be cast with likeable actors.

I don't mean for Trudy and Keith to be liars. In the stylized farce world of the play, I mean for the awful things that happened to them in their childhoods to be true. I also want us to feel they're kind of sweet at their core, and even mean well. But then when later on they maim and kill, I'm with Betty — a bad childhood doesn't give you the excuse to kill or maim people.

(I'm not judging abused wives in life who sometimes kill their husbands after years of hideous violence and after failed attempts to get away. They may or may not be legally justified, depending on the specific cases, but I certainly have sympathy. But the play does judge people killing (or maiming) other people out of revenge, or because they were mistreated.)

TRUDY. The part of Trudy needs someone able to make Trudy's excessive talking funny and not tedious. One of the clues is that Trudy's mind is a jumble and jumps from one thing to another *very quickly.* That's one requirement for the part — the ability to talk quickly and charmingly (still making the connections between things, but just very fast). Another requirement is that she seem kind of nice and also emotionally needy (anxious to connect to someone — to Keith, to Buck, until he becomes impossible).

Trudy also has to have some genuine anger and upset about how she's been psychologically and sexually abused. The actress has to have a truthful psychological basis; yet it also needs not to be hit too heavily, or wallowed in, because this is not a *realistic* play about sexual abuse. The actress needs to be serious enough so we know we're not being asked to find sexual abuse funny, or to dismiss it; but her acting has to be "light" enough so that we don't feel we're in a serious play. We're in a different kind of world — a bit cartoonish, a bit *Candide*-like (with Betty the Candide figure), a screwball comedy where terrible things happen. But not cartoonish acting — a special kind that is real psychologically but still has a comic spin to it. (1930s screwball comedy acting gives good examples of the kind of acting that can work.)

Our original Trudy, Julie Lund, was terrific in the part, funny and inventive. I was also very grateful for how she played the end of Act One, from her rape to her act of mutilation. The rape scene is the trickiest in the play; and I'll mention it more below.

KEITH. Writing the part of Keith, the type of actor I thought of was a young, boyish, sweet type. Uncomfortable around people, seemingly without any hostile impulses in him. Like a young Matthew Broderick, though more shy, less spunk.

When we auditioned for the part, for some reason we saw a lot of tall, gangly actors for the part, many of them excellent. And I started to think of another way to go as a young Anthony Perkins. If you re-watch Anthony Perkins in the Hitchcock classic *Psycho*, in the first part of the movie Perkins (who plays a crazy killer) is incredibly sweet and charming, very genuinely so. It's a very good prototype for the part.

Nat DeWolf, whom we cast as Keith, wasn't tall and gangly like Perkins; and he wasn't quite as boyishly soft as some of the Keiths I originally thought of. But he is a very gifted comic actor; he absolutely had a sweetness and shyness at his core, and his imagination took him to many quirky choices. (One of my favorites was late in the play when he's about to light the match to blow up the house and kill everyone ... Betty yells, "Keith, don't strike the match," and his response is "But I want to." The conventional line reading (which would be fine too) would be "let me have my way, I'm going to do what I want." Nat's line reading had a softer shading as if Betty was worried that he was doing something he didn't want to do, and he was gently assuring her, no, no, I would find blowing up the house to be very a pleasant thing. ("But I want to.")

Whatever Keith does with body parts and/or with Mr. Vanislaw is meant to remain vague — at worst, it's horrible; at best, it might be very, very strange. But let's not think about it too much.

I loved how Nat, inviting Mr. Vanislaw back to his room, seemed to have a kind of gentle crush on him. It seemed oddly innocent. Keith is insane; but I think he is indeed oddly innocent.

THE RAPE SCENE (and the scene that follows). The offstage rape of Trudy is the scariest part of the play to direct or perform, and it's scary for the audience as well, because they feel very, very uncomfortable.

The rape has to be disturbing, and a truly bad thing, because I want Trudy to be emotionally justified in wanting to strike out against her attacker — at the same time I (and Betty and I hope you) disapprove of what she does. But she has to have been truly sinned against.

During the rape itself, because the play has been kind of giddy and clearly comic up until this point, the audience doesn't know what emotions to feel.

Our fabulously talented Mrs. Siezmagraff, Kristine Nielsen, was so endlessly inventive and so innately funny that in some early previews the director and I realized that she was making a number of acting choices during the rape that were funny; and the audience felt mixed up and upset at seemingly being asked to find anything during that section as funny.

So we asked her to simplify her choices during this section (without losing her character, of course; she's still out of it, half-drunk, half not knowing what's happening, half immediately blaming Trudy) so that the audience no longer felt it was being asked to laugh.

They were still uncomfortable during this section — I think they have to be, you just don't quite know where the play's going at this point. It's the "car accident" portion of the play.

But Julie Lund's interpretation of the scene once she came out of the room, after the rape, helped a great deal — she was clearly angry and upset, it had a clear emotional truth to it. You saw that the actress took her violation seriously, and you saw that you weren't supposed to find her suffering funny or negligible. However, she also didn't push the upset too far, as you might be allowed to do in a realistic scene about after a rape.

Her fairly realistic anger relieved us in the audience, we had our bearings back. Then when she stalked offstage with a knife, and Mrs. Siezmagraff mildly said, "Be nice now," totally disconnected from Trudy's anger or from what any normal person would worry about regarding a knife — somehow the play's strange, skewed comic tone started to reassert itself.

When Trudy then returned with the unattached member, and she and her mother start bickering about how to handle the situation, and Mrs. Siezmagraff has many of her inappropriate/inadequate responses (like, "I invite a guest into this house, and this is how he is treated") — well, most audiences started laughing a lot then; we were back in the strange comic world of the play once more. The excess of the play — the mutilation, the beheading — had reasserted itself in theatrical terms; and most audiences laughed, knowing they were in a skewed, comic world where horrible things happened. But it was a play; it was actors; it wasn't really happening — and for most of us, that allows us the distance to laugh and to think.

THE BLOOD. In production, I felt strongly that I didn't want to see blood in Act One — I didn't want it on Mr. Vanislaw's rain-coat when Keith wears the raincoat after the beheading; I didn't want it on Keith's hands or person. Yes, I know if you actually beheaded someone, you'd probably get covered in blood — but I didn't want to look at Keith covered in blood for the next hour; it's not that kind of play; it's not about the horror of murders. And I didn't want to see Trudy's knife, all bloody after the fact; and I didn't want to see whatever weapon Keith used to cut off the head.

By leaving out the blood, you let the play remain kind of stylized — they talk about the awful things that happen, but we are not visually reminding the audience about the horrors of physical violence. It's too strong — it would trump the play's verbal jokes and ongoing logic.

Along the same lines, the first prop to represent the cut-off penis was all bloody; and I asked them to redo it without blood. (And also no jokes about choosing a prop that's either too big or too small.)

The director then came up with the idea, along with the actors, of barely showing the severed member. Trudy stalked back onstage after attacking Mr. Vanislaw and was carrying something in her upstage hand.

Then when she handed it to her mother, Mrs. Siezmagraff held it in the palm of her hand (somewhat cupped) and said, "I don't understand, what is it?" Then when she realized, she raced about the stage in a confused manner, trying to think where to put it, what to do with it. When she said, "Keith, put this on ice," she handed it to Keith, and he stood staring at it ... again, with his hands kind of cupped so we saw it but also didn't see it.

Then, as per the script, Trudy grabs it back, wishing to throw it into the ocean. Her mother tries to stop her, and then the director had Trudy suddenly shake the member at her mother in anger on the line "He raped me!" And the audience screamed with laughter and discomfort; it was the first real clear look at the prop they'd gotten. Then Mrs. Siezmagraff grabbed it back and put it in the freezer.

I agree — there's more than one way to do a scene. But for what it's worth, my preference is that you don't go for showing blood (and especially not for gross out kind of blood), and that you also are "subtle" with the use of the severed penis prop. (Note: We did use some blood late in the play, after Keith and Trudy behead Buck. Now Keith's raincoat was somewhat bloody; and Trudy's hands were also somewhat bloody, and she was wiping them on a towel. But now we were at the end of the play, and the house is going to blow up in a few minutes; so the tone of the play allows us to be more grotesque.)

MR. VANISLAW. This part seems tricky to cast. In some early readings of the play, I saw some good actors play the exhibitionist side of Mr. Vanislaw in a way that ended up feeling dark and too creepy. Guy Boyd, who was so excellent as a fuzzy, illogical senator in my play *Sex and Longing*, was terrific as Mr. Vanislaw too — he has a goofiness to him that comes from some sweet-natured side of his nature; and the way he would gallumph about the stage, flashing people with his raincoat, was certainly not "nice" behavior, but it was nutty behavior, rather than sinister or dark or innately scary. He was an inappropriate little boy who has now grown up, but still gives in to his most uncensored, inappropriate impulses.

THE VOICES. The three actors cast need to have an ability and a skill to speak in unison so they can be understood. Thus sometime in rehearsal, they and the director have to decide on what their unison line readings are — if two voices emphasize one word, and the third voice emphasizes another word, the audience will not hear the sentence properly. So they must choose their vocal inflections in advance, and then perform them in synch.

When the Voices arrive in Act Two and start speaking singly, and have definite characters, then certainly idiosyncratic line readings are more acceptable (if they fit the line, of course).

We chose to cast one of the Voices as black. The ethnic background of the Voices is not important, though we had some fears if we cast more than one, audiences might decide we were saying the Voices represented minority groups, rather than represented a total cross section of America (hard to do with just three people).

The Voices and their costume came about from the concept of a laugh track.

For a long time I've wanted to write a play in which there was a laugh track; my initial impulse behind that was simply how strange it would be to walk about your living room or kitchen, and have the sounds of audience response sort of "in the air" around you. Kind of like watching *I Love Lucy* and forgetting our knowledge that it was performed in front of an audience, but instead believing there were secret eyes and ears and voices that somehow inhabited the air in the Ricardo apartment, and let out very loud laughter and whispering when they were amused or surprised, etc. etc.

Then as I was writing the play, I started to want the laugh track to speak — in unison, as a kind of Greek Chorus. (The concept of a Greek Chorus, in modern times, has always struck me as funny; it's a concept that strikes us odd nowadays, talking in unison.) And initially I had them responding as a kind of "normal" audience; and early on, they are seemingly disturbed by some of the characters' behavior.

In Act Two, I wanted them to do more. And, envisioning their boredom after the gruesome highlights of Act One, I had them verbalize what they wanted the characters to do. Out of boredom, they wanted Betty to look at the penis in the freezer again. Then, as time goes by in the play, I have them want more and more extreme things.

So in some ways, the theme embodied by the voices doesn't become clear until Act Two — though Act One, luckily, functions as a story, where we meet who the characters are and understand how they get to do the things they do.

For what it's worth, I don't exempt myself as a viewer from some of what I accuse the public of giving in to — I became riveted by the Clarence Thomas/Anita Hill hearings, for instance, initially because I cared about who was being appointed to the Supreme Court (and was angered at Thomas' lack of first class credentials and by the Republicans' cynical manipulation of appointing a black conservative, to make it hard for liberals to criticize him, they thought). However, once the lurid details of pubic hair on Coke cans and the subsequent smearing of Anita Hill followed — and the possible smearing of him, too — well, it was an extremely disturbing public event.

Yet, it was also wildly entertaining like a really gripping movie — it was hard to tell who was telling the truth, the various senators fulfilled their roles like cleverly cast supporting actors (Senator Heflin, with a thick Southern accent, asking Ms. Hill if she was a "sconed" woman, meaning "scorned").

I chose in *Betty's* to focus on lurid personal cases, and left out the ones with political overtones (like the Hill/Thomas hearings) or with racial overtones (like the O.J. case or Hill/Thomas again) because politics and race deserve full plays or considerations, and as topics were larger than this play could handle.

But the way that life's tragedies can become entertainment on television has become a rather depressing constant in our lives.

Back to the play a sec — how to costume the Voices is a real challenge. Stage directions aside, I want to say: They are not three distinct people who appear from the ceiling. It's odder than that. I start with the idea that a Laugh Track is an entity ... a group who somehow lives in your ceiling or in the air, and they follow everything you do and they laugh when something's funny. Then if they start to talk, well, yes they contain some distinct personalities, but they don't go home separately at night, they always stay together — in my head, they are some sort of "entity." So when they show up, with three distinct heads (and personalities accompanying the heads), nonetheless their bodies are joined at the hip (as we did in the Playwrights production), or maybe they all share one body.

So it's an interesting challenge how to design them. Go to it!

THE SET. The interior of the beach house should be pleasant, airy, inviting. It is not wealthy or chic, or meant to imply any "fancy" beach areas. Some of the decorating choices can be corny (like paintings of ships and so on), but overall it should look like a nice place.

There are so many doors! Our wonderful designer, Thomas Lynch, managed to design a set with five doors for five bedrooms, with another door for an entrance from outside, and with a sliding glass door leading to a deck. And somehow on the medium-sized stage, it still looked pleasing and inviting.

In his set there was a small hallway that actually had four doorways off it (the door to Betty's room was slightly inside the room, at the beginning of the hall), and then there was a doorway on the other side of the room for Keith's room.

At the end of the hallway (upstage) was the door to the outside (presumably where you could park your car); this door had adjustable glass slats (for letting air in).

So in terms of stage picture, you didn't really see all the doors off the hallway unless people were coming in and out of them; you saw instead the upstage door to the outside. And it was sufficiently upstage that you didn't really focus on it too much either. It was the furniture downstage, and the kitchen area and the glass door leading to the deck that tended to be dominant. (And those areas are where most of the action takes place.)

I can imagine smaller stages, or thrust stages, where it would be harder to design a set that could somehow include all these doors. So I want to say that I think, if you had to, you could design a set where some of the doors (and rooms) were offstage: Buck's room and Mrs. Siezmagraff's room could both be offstage; Betty's could be too, if you had to (though I'd prefer not). The doors to Trudy's room and to Keith's room have to be onstage, though.

THE BEACH. The audience lives in the beach house set for almost the entire play. When the house blows up and we switch to the beach, however you do it, my main wish is that we totally lose the house and change the look a great deal.

At Playwrights Horizons, the entire beach house was on a wagon and was able to move quite far upstage (manually, by stage hands). When Keith lit the match, Nicholas Martin had the actors freeze, added the sound of explosions, added the lights going wild (with lots of orange), and we in the audience watched the beach house move away from us — almost like a film still that was receding into the distance. It was very satisfying, and very elegant. (And also very unexpected.)

Then the light flashes switched to rather blinding lights out

81

toward the audience; and while that happened, a black drop was lowered in front of the now receded beach house; and a simple set piece suggesting dunes on the beach was put onstage. And the dunes had grasses and reeds growing out of them, in silhouette. And it's night, so the lighting was blueish and not too bright (though with a special on Betty; I don't want her in darkness). The dim lighting meant that the dune backdrop didn't have to be too realistically done. The silhouette (against dark blue night sky) kind of did the work.

If you have a very deep stage, getting rid of the beach house entirely is probably possible. If you don't have a deep stage, you probably can't get rid of it easily (and at Playwrights it only went upstage, it didn't disappear totally; the drop came down in front of it about midstage).

Whatever solution you come up with, do what you can to have the beach look totally different from what's come before; and to have the house disappear from our view as best you can.

SOME MISCELLANEOUS NOTES

BUCK. From some early readings, I see a clear trap in playing Buck. It's important the actor not play Buck as stupid; or worse, somehow play Buck, all the while looking for ways to *indicate* to us that he knows Buck is a jerk or is inappropriate or is a sexist pig. We'll get all that from the script; the actor doesn't have to look for ways to communicate the very thing the script has already made clear.

Instead the actor playing Buck should play that he thinks he's just fine, he likes life, he likes sex, he likes women. When Troy Sostillio first auditioned for Buck, the main thing he played was that he was excited to meet Betty, he thought she was attractive, he tended to stand a bit too close to her, but with real charm; he hoped they'd have sex. He didn't play: "I'm a jerk, I'm a creep, I'm a sexist." The character was that as written. So he played instead: "I like women; oh, look, this Betty seems nice, hi, Betty, want a beer?" Etc.

A STRAY LINE. In Act One, Scene 5, Trudy goes off to Keith's bedroom holding a knife and revenges herself on Mr. Vanislaw. A second later Keith comes running out of the room and says to Mrs. Siezmagraff, "You better call the police." Her response is: "Again? I can't keep calling the police. They'll think I'm a crank."

This is a very crazy line; no one has called the police before in the play. Kristine Nielsen never asked me about it, but just did it with no problem. Once in conversation it came up and she said, well, Mrs. Siezmagraff is remembering from earlier in the play when Betty asks if they should call the police regarding their suspicions about Keith and his hatbox, and Mrs. Siezmagraff says no, they shouldn't, Keith might "misunderstand" such an action on their part. And so, with extremely fuzzy Mrs. Siezmagraff logic, she emotionally feels they did call the police earlier — or at least talked about it — and so she feels real resistance to calling them, as she puts it, "again."

Nutty; but I like that Kristine got it without my explaining it. And that is what I meant.

THE TRIAL. This sequence, where Mrs. Siezmagraff acts out a whole trial to placate the Voices, was great fun for me to write. Also, I wrote it before the play's first public reading, knowing that Kristine N. was going to read the part; so I wrote it knowing of, and inspired by, her great comic facility.

I do think there are lots of ways to do the scene, most likely, but one pointer I'd like to give: Even though Leslie Abramson (the amusingly brash lawyer who represented the Menendez Brothers) is mentioned in the play, it is a mistake to try to imitate her as the defense attorney. The story of the trial needs to move along swiftly and clearly, and both Mrs. Siezmagraff and the Irish maid have a lot to act; the defense attorney (and the bailiff, more briefly seen) need just to be businesslike and lawyerly, to make their points move along. It doesn't help the "flow" to try to give them too much character.

Plus, Leslie Abramson is a fascinating figure, and were I to try to write her, I'd need to give her her own emotions and style, none of which is included in the straight-forward writing of the defense attorney in *Betty's*. (Kristine chose to flatten her voice slightly as the defense attorney; that worked, and I also think just using your normal voice with lawyerly inflections would also work.)

THE LAST SCENE. I wrote the final scene for a couple of reasons. I greatly felt the need to blow up all the characters and the house — they'd become insane past rehabilitation, and I felt the need as an author and an audience to be rid of them. But I didn't like the idea of just ending it that way; and I felt Betty somehow deserved to escape too. And I wanted Betty to try calm herself down, to begin the process of overcoming her trauma; and to help the audience calm down after the frenetic craziness of the play and its upsetting, manic events.

The last scene, emotionally, is almost like a "cool down" after a particularly ferocious workout.

Kellie Overbey initially did the speech exactly as I envisioned it, calm, vulnerable, in need of solace, finding it in the sound of her breathing and in listening to the ocean.

In early previews though, we found that Betty had gotten to a place of calm almost too soon, the audience didn't get there with her at the same time. And it was clear that the speech needed to begin more speedy-like, more upset still from the murders and mayhem and the explosion. And that Betty's brain is almost on overdrive as she tries to think what her part in it was, and should she feel guilty, and what she should do in the future to protect herself from scary people. It's somewhere midway (when she says, "the house seems to be smoldering somewhere behind me in the distance") that she calms down, hears the ocean and finds solace in it.

Sometimes I could see Kellie's face suddenly lose tension as she heard the ocean … and I would feel such relief as well, also losing tension.

So that's what I intend.

TERRIFIC PRODUCTION. Writing a play and then putting it on is such a complicated process; and it's hard for all the elements to come together right. Sometimes they don't come together at all, and it's a mess. More often, some things come together, others don't, and it's a partial success, partial mess.

I was so, so happy and proud of the production of *Betty's Summer Vacation* at Playwrights Horizons. There are nine characters in the play, and each one was beautifully played — Julie Lund as Trudy, Nat DeWolf as Keith, Troy Sostillio as Buck, Guy Boyd as Mr. Vanislaw, Jack Ferver as quirky Voice #1, Geneva Carr as sometimes gracious, sometimes vicious Voice #2, and Godfrey L. Simmons, Jr. as intelligent, sometimes forceful/macho Voice #3.

Kellie Overbey first performed Betty at a reading at the Ojai Playwrights Festival, and I thought she was wonderful; and I was so happy she got to do the play at Playwrights Horizons; Kellie captured Betty's humanity throughout the play, and her comic reactions to the craziness around her gave the play the grounding I always felt the part of Betty needed to give.

And Kristine Nielsen had a triumph as Mrs. Siezmagraff (and how I wish you'd seen her if you didn't). Kristine and I met as fellow actors in a not successful production of *Ubu* at Lincoln Center (though I noted she always made her scene work regardless). And I had seen her be excellent numerous times, and was knocked out by her Obie-winning performance in Constance Congdon's excellent play *Dog Opera*; and then I had seen her tear up the theatre doing John Augustine's funny and poignant *Rebecca Ruth* monologue. So I was thrilled to have her enter the crazy world of Mrs. Siezmagraff; she detonated her scenes, gave a motor to the whole play, and was just overall kind of thrilling.

And it was all overseen masterfully by director Nicholas Martin, who made every day's rehearsal fun and playful; and who guided the actors and oversaw the designers to a beautifully realized production; and who had an unerring eye and ear for how far to go with the comedy, what tone it should be, what pace, etc. etc.

A very happy production experience for me, and for the audience. Thanks to all.

And that's all for my notes. I've left out some topics, but I can't and shouldn't just go on and on and on with notes. So I hope these are helpful.

Christopher Durang
June 2000